AF342224

CHRISTIANITY AND THE NARROW WAY

CHRISTIANITY AND THE NARROW WAY

Roy C. Jarnagin

Exposition Press   *Smithtown, New York*

To my wife, Madaline, for her
unfailing love and support

All canonical Scripture quotations are from the King James Version of the Holy Bible.

First Edition

Library of Congress Catalog Card Number: 81-69728

ISBN 0-682-49832-7

Printed in the United States of America

CONTENTS

Acknowledgment

I wish to acknowledge with deepest gratitude my debt to Dr. Maurice L. Rider—great thinker, scholar, philosopher, and friend—who took a personal interest in the development of this work.

Foreword

A wily old wag I knew once said, "Superstition is the other man's religion." And then, in deference to his audience and his own good health, he added: "Unless he is a Jew or a Christian!"

The author of *Christianity and the Narrow Way* must see the amusing as well as the ironic side of religious controversy, else he could not have written this splendid and many-faceted book. But he very properly insists that there is more than humor and irony in our failure to fit our faith to reality. So long as we persist in saying "the thing which was not" about the origin of our convictions, so long will vicious cults spring up and flourish among us. The Judeo-Christian pots cannot justly call the cultic kettles black.

Roy Jarnagin was brought up on sound Presbyterian doctrine, which (I am told by members of the faith) is about as Christian as one can get. He therefore has the advantage of knowing whereof he speaks and, unlike H. L. Mencken and Bertrand Russell, has not had to smell the incense from across the street.

But living in the faith and growing up in it is not enough to understand it. Mr. Jarnagin has read widely and deeply in the literature of all the major religions, and as the mastery of one language helps in learning another, so does the knowledge of other religions improve the understanding of one's own. The evidence upon which Mr. Jarnagin has built his book has been accumulating for a long time. Textual criticism and scholarly study of the Bible began in the Middle Ages and is not, as many suppose, a product of recent philosophical and scientific thought. The mass of evidence which sifts truth from falsehood, history from myth, and ethics from propaganda in the Bible is monumental, impartial, and venerable. Mr. Jarnagin has read widely in it, and the pages of his book show how well he has wrung the truth from historical and textual accounts.

Also apparent is the deftness with which he has ordered his facts and presented his arguments. His style is lean and precise. It has a succinctness which pleases the careful reader and an economy of words that snaps the casual reader to attention. One must read his prose cadences with the intensity one usually reserves for poetry. Some would call it hard reading because it lacks the facile phrase and the expected cliché of the slicks, but if the words move slowly, the sense they bear is substantial and vibrant. It is no disgrace to reread this book with half the meticulous care with which it was written. Here, indeed, are "infinite riches in a little room."

Christianity and the Narrow Way can be read in several different ways. It is first of all a serious criticism of the popular concept of Christianity. There are churchmen liberal enough to say that no thinking person actually believes the myths and dogma Mr. Jarnagin so roundly condemns—that he is systematically beating a dead horse. At the other end of the church the wardens of the superstitious fringe will look uneasily to their arsenal of prayer, propaganda, and censorship. I wish I could honestly say to these good people that this is a dangerous book. But it isn't. There is nothing in it to lead the innocent astray or to confirm the wicked in their ways. If one man can guess another's motives, I would say that Mr. Jarnagin wants to purge religion of its nonsense so that it might get on with the business of helping people live the good life. Why he chose to help Christians and Jews rather than Mohammedans, Buddhists, or Hindus I do not know. Perhaps he thought the plight of the Christian more urgent.

The lover of satire will not be disappointed in what he finds here. Mr. Jarnagin's ironic thrust comes mainly in the fictional portion of his book. His new story of the nativity and his explanation of the Deluge light up more clearly the anomalies of the biblical accounts, but the Bible is not the sole mark for his mordant wit. The whole congeries of UFO hardware and personnel gets into the act to the amusement of the skeptic and the romantic delight of the science-fiction buff. The serious reader sees in the Andorian super race a vision of what mankind could be like if men were persuaded to follow the teachings of Jesus of Nazareth. The fictional (Andorian) Jesus is a fraud with the very best of intentions who fails in his mission after the classic manner of most religious and civic leaders. The fictional portion of the book ends with mankind about where it always was, but the reader is a bit more wary of any social panacea created and maintained by dogma and deceit.

Am I implying that the book is a plea for an honest religion? Mr. Jarnagin is not an unreasonable person! He does, however, suggest ever so gently that the reader ponder his very own answers to questions such as these: In Exodus 23:13, why does the god of Abraham, Isaac, and Jacob command the Israelites to "make no mention of the name of other gods, neither let it be heard out of thy mouth"? Does Yahweh know that gods pine away and die when they go unmentioned and unremembered? Is God a reliable and predictable force, like gravity, the behavior of which all men agree upon, or is It like justice, a concept existing only in men's minds and differing in character from man to man? Which came first, man or religion? Are Christians and others sustained and renewed by their religion, or is it they who keep their religion going and their gods alive? Why should there be any difference of opinion about who or what God is? If God is capable of manifesting himself to *some* men, why not to *all* men? Why do all faiths have priests, prophets, and pretenders as go-betweens to explain their god to the common people and to see that the gifts of believers reach the off-hours depository at the bank?

And Mr. Jarnagin also suggests that there is room for another branch of the Christian faith stripped of all its trappings of false propaganda and superstition. He suggests the nature of that way of life, and he hints at what personal satisfactions await those who embrace such a philosophy. But just as sure as Jesus taught that the kingdom of heaven is within us, so does this book affirm that the power and the glory also have their existence in the minds of men. And it behooves every man to heed his neighbor's insights, to research the world of record through book, artifact, and fossil, to synthesize new information in search of more meaningful truths, and to exercise at all times his natural birthright—his freedom to choose between horse sense and faith, between tradition and observation, between sectarianism and an almost universal code of secular morality and decency, between the Everlasting Figment of the Communal Imagination and his own concept of universal order.

Here I have tried to set down some of the things a manuscript reading of this book has meant to me. Some early prejudices from my Methodist childhood and a congenital insensitivity to the beauty of holiness have blinded me, I am sure, to much that is good in these pages. What I have missed, others will see and magnify, for there is literally no end to the implications in a work of this stature. It is a book that invites discussion—serious discussion—as among study groups in churches of the better sort. Indeed, it could do no harm in any church or synagogue where the Holy Bible is regularly read and discussed.

The world will grow in spirit and in truth during the decades ahead, and as for this volume, time, experience, and new perspectives will enrich its meaning. "Behold, how great a matter a little fire kindleth!"

Maurice L. Rider

Fairhope, Alabama
January 1980

"Enter ye in at the strait gate: for wide is the gate, and broad is the way, that leadeth to destruction, and many there be which go in thereat: Because strait is the gate, and narrow is the way, which leadeth unto life, and few there be that find it." (Matt. 7:13-14)

PART ONE

Reason is the triumph of the intellect, faith of the heart; and whether the one or the other shall best illuminate the dark mysteries of our being, they are only to be despaired of who care not to explore.—James Schouler

1

The Anatomy of Religious Beliefs

Scratch the Christian and you find the pagan—spoiled.—I. Zangwill

In the twentieth century Christianity has become the most popular religion on earth. At the same time the unrealistic nature of its beliefs has alienated many sincere seekers while prompting the serious investigator to question its relevance to the human experience and to reexamine the entire concept of religion.

Through the ages mankind's religious urge has found expression in a bewildering variety of beliefs, ideas, and practices. But a common thread runs through them all: the attempt of a finite mind to explain the infinities of space and time, to deal with the awesome forces of nature, to fathom the mysteries of existence, and come to terms with its own mortality.

However, the primitive mind, steeped in ignorance and superstition, was unable to cope with such profound abstractions. Taking the easy course, it turned away from these frightening uncertainties and concocted a simpler reality. It was a reality controlled by a god or gods possessed of unlimited powers, yet subject to human frailties and thus amenable to manipulation.

The early pagan worshiped and placated gods made in his image and after his likeness—magnified reflections of himself. Historically there were the numerous Roman and Greek gods on the one hand and the Hebrew Jehovah on the other. Today the religious spectrum is just as diffuse. At one end is Hinduism, which has endured for 5,000 years on a diet of polytheism, reincarnation, and karma. At the other end is Confucianism, more a religious philosophy than a religion, which has survived for more than 2,000 years without any god at all by teaching that man is good and possesses free will, and that virtue is its own reward. Somewhere in between lies Christianity, now in its second millennium, which worships a Triune God and declares man to be essentially evil. Together these disparate belief systems claim 1.66 billion adherents, or nearly one-half of the world's population.

Some writers have asserted that fear of one kind or another is the basis of all religion. If fear is its foundation, then its cornerstone is the virtually universal desire to find a scapegoat for all wrongdoing—a guiltless individual who will suffer the consequences of our sins. Accordingly, several religions have embraced the concept of "remission of sins."

It was an ancient doctrine that "without the shedding of blood (of the innocent), there is no remission of sin." It punished the innocent that the guilty might escape. It murdered the gods that man might sin with impunity.

The propitiation of God by bloody sacrifices dominated the pagan and Jewish worlds. Religion consisted of placating the gods by gifts and sacrifices. If the gods were hostile, they could be bribed; if they were angry, they could be placated by gifts.

The belief in a man-god who would die and thus save the world was common to all pagan religions except that of Judaism.

Bel-Merodach of Assyria and Babylon was the son of Hea (God) and was revered as the Prince of Light, the Conqueror of the Dragon, the Redeemer of Mankind and Giver of Life. He was a savior-god who died and conquered death, descended into the underworld, broke the gates thereof, and returned to the living, having released the dead from captivity. His resurrection occurred three days after his death, and in both Babylon and Phoenicia a kind of Good Friday and Easter were observed in his honor.

Osiris of the Egyptians died and arose to new life.

Mithras (sun god), in the Mithraic religion, was the mediator between God and man. Born of a virgin, he was called the "Righteous Incarnate"—the vice-regent of God on earth; the judge on the day of resurrection; the savior of mankind who was to lead the good in their battle against Ahriman, the evil one.

Mithraism, which was brought to Rome in 68 B.C., was prevalent throughout the Roman Empire, especially in the army. During the second and third centuries of our era it was a rival of Christianity but was suppressed in A.D. 378. Examples of man-god saviors are found in pagan religions throughout Europe, Asia, Africa, and the Americas.

Propitiation of God by blood sacrifices and the transfer of righteousness from the innocent to the guilty was the central theme of these pagan doctrines. Such beliefs must have been known to several of the Apostles, particularly to a man of education like St. Paul. With such a background how easy it would have been after a few years to find it necessary to alter the simple teachings of the man Jesus so as to bring them into line with the prevalent idea of God and what was expected of his children.

It would appear, therefore, that all these old doctrines and certain of the Jewish ones were gathered together and fitted around Jesus to make him conform to the accepted beliefs. And, so, Christianity became a later version of ancient doctrines. At this writing more than one-third of the planet's inhabitants has been converted to some form of Christianity. This being so, the question arises: How can a race whose science has produced television, computers, and space probes content itself with a warmed-over version of primitive religious fabrications?

This question, with its paradoxes and implications, will be examined in the following pages. From the material thus presented we can infer that for thousands of years the spiritual development of Homo sapiens has been mired in the sands of gullibility and wishful thinking. And this will lead to the realization that Christianity is a religion of self-delusion, that it is a system of belief based on a spurious reality.

However, this book should not be construed as a diatribe on Christianity. Any religion by whatever name, promulgating the same doctrine, would be as vulnerable to the challenge of intellect. Any savior by whatever name—Bel-Merodach, Osiris, Mithras, or Christ—would serve as a crutch for a species crippled by irresponsibility and self-delusion. Such a system of belief by any other name would still be a cop-out.

It is not the writer's intent to disparage any religion or to undermine any particular structure of faith. His only purpose is to search for the truth in whatever guise it may appear, and perhaps in the process to liberate reason from the shackles of emotion and credulity. If the quest takes us into modes of thought abhorrent to the orthodox mind, so be it. Orthodoxy in thought and belief, particularly the variety that advocates the forgiveness of sins via a sacrificial scapegoat, is in large measure responsible for the kind of world we live in today.

Just as it originally embraced the idea that planet Earth is flat and the center of creation, Christian orthodoxy is still wedded to the outmoded conception of a mechanistic universe. Advanced thinkers in physics and astronomy are now in general agreement that the cosmos is more like a great thought than like a great machine.

If this is true, it follows that everything was created by and is controlled by thought. So who is the Thinker? That is a question all the religions of the world have been unable to answer with any degree of cogency despite their involutional reasoning in support of an anthropomorphic creator.

Yet deep within his being Everyman knows intuitively that he lives in a mental world. If he takes the time to consider, he realizes that all action, all accomplishment begin with a thought, an idea. He cannot but conclude that all motivation is mental. It could hardly be otherwise in a cosmos that functions through mind-generated force fields.

Life itself, which manifests in the material world of the five senses, has to have a nonmaterial origin in a realm beyond the space-time world of physical sensations. And this brings us to a better understanding of death. It is not the atheist's one-way ticket to oblivion, nor is it the religionist's dead-end street to a judgmental God. Instead, death can be recognized as the return portion of a continuous journey, marking the liberation of life's indestructible spirit from its physical cocoon.

Around 400 B.C. Plato, one of the most remarkable intellects of all time, held that there are two worlds: the world of appearance and the world of reality. He asserted that the world of appearance is known by means of the five senses and is full of illusion, change, and decay; but the real world is one of eternal, changeless "Ideas," which can be known only by the intellect. His contemporary, Aristotle, believed that there must exist a perfect, nonmaterial, and changeless being from which all "Ideas" ultimately derive. And this being is God.

But the Golden Age of Greek philosophy, with its vigorous use of reason to explore the essential nature of things, appealed only to an intellectual elite. There was nothing in it for ordinary men and women.

Four centuries were to pass before this two-world concept would be presented in simpler terms directed to the ordinary people of the times. That was the real mission of Jesus Christ. Throughout his career this greatest of mystics challenged all formal and legalistic religion, calling upon the common man to acknowledge the mental kingdom within and its dominion over the outer world of appearance. Time after time Jesus demonstrated the power of thought. One such instance is mentioned almost incidentally in the eleventh chapter of

Mark's Gospel where the Master berated the fig tree for not bearing fruit. Later it was discovered the tree had withered and died.

This mental power was further emphasized by the Nazarene as related in Mark 11:23-24, when he told his disciples: "For verily I say unto you, That whosoever shall say unto this mountain, Be thou removed, and be thou cast into the sea; and shall not doubt in his heart, but shall believe that those things which he saith shall come to pass; he shall have whatsoever he saith. Therefore I say unto you, What things soever ye desire, when ye pray [commune with the creative power within], believe that ye receive them, and ye shall have them."

Again, in John 7:24, Jesus said: "Judge not according to the appearance, but judge righteous judgment." Here he is restating the distinction drawn by Plato between the world of appearance, which is known by means of the five senses, and the real world of eternal, changeless ideas. Righteous, or right, judgment requires that we recognize the mental origin of all manifestation.

This extraordinary man used every means at his command to make the two-world concept understandable to all who had "ears to hear and eyes to see." His cosmotheistic use of the term "the Kingdom of God is within you" was a clear reference to the creative power residing in consciousness, which fashioned the universe and stands ready to serve any human need. Yet his simple teachings were so distorted by the priesthood their real meaning has been lost. As a result, the Christian has disavowed the message while deifying the messenger.

It is still true that men worship what they do not understand. And that is the ultimate irony.

2

Christian Doctrine and Traditions

When once a man is determined to believe, the very absurdity of the doctrine does but confirm him in his faith.—Junius

A visitor from outer space, immune to the infectious religious fevers of Earth, would doubtless conclude that a belief system such as Christianity sabotages the spiritual development of all believers, and, further, that it constitutes the greatest disservice to mankind, converted and infidel alike, ever perpetrated on any species. Its promise of "salvation" through the suffering and death of a surrogate is so insidious that even the atheist becomes convinced he can get something for nothing, that the law of cause and effect somehow does not operate in the Christian's reality.

Such a reality concept contradicts all that is taught in the school of hard knocks. In the natural world every creature must suffer the consequences of a blunder or wrongful action. Nature is terribly unforgiving of any infraction of its laws, or "sinfulness" in the religious vernacular. The foolish fish swallows the hook and ends up in the frying pan, not a surrogate *pisces*. The unwary sparrow becomes a meal for the hawk, not some substitute fowl. The careless hunter draws a painfully burned hand from the campfire, not one of his more cautious companions.

Because of his faith in a so-called savior, the Christian can immerse himself in the fires of sin with the comforting assurance that the savior will be burned in his stead and that he, as a wrongdoer, will escape the consequences of his acts. On any level of thought this is a travesty on Everyman's innate sense of justice. As Harold W. Percival put it, "If individuals can be relieved of the consequences of their sins by the sacrifice of another, there is no reason for a belief in justice."

The truth—which the Christian prefers to ignore—is that no fault can be atoned for; no one can escape the consequences of his actions by any means. If such were possible, man would learn nothing from experience and life on this plane would serve no purpose.

Although Christianity is out of touch with reality, as the psychiatrist might put it, this belief system has flourished around the globe for 2,000 years, and no doubt will continue to do so until it is finally hoist on its own petard. Can such popularity be deserved? Indeed it can and the reason is a simple one. The architects of Christianity have pandered to the mental laziness, irresponsibility, and wishful thinking that have characterized the human race since the time of Adam.

In short, it is a theology that encourages the tendency in all of us to follow the path of least resistance, to swallow and follow rather than to think things out for ourselves. Let's take a closer look at this belief system which holds over a billion subjects in thrall.

Its basic doctrine is summed up in what is known as the Apostles' Creed. There are a number of variations, but they do not alter the general structure of belief. One version of this dogma, the Presbyterian, was engraved upon the impressionable young mind of the writer so indelibly that more than fifty years later he can repeat it verbatim.

1. I believe in God the Father Almighty,
2. and in Jesus Christ, His only-begotten Son, our Lord,
3. who was conceived by the Holy Ghost and born of the Virgin Mary,
4. who was crucified under Pontius Pilate and buried;
5. He descended into hell;
6. on the third day He rose from the dead,
7. ascended into heaven,
8. and sitteth on the right hand of God the Father Almighty,
9. from whence He shall come to judge the quick and the dead;
10. and in the Holy Ghost;
11. the Holy Catholic Church;
12. the communion of saints,
13. the remission of sins;
14. the resurrection of the body and the life everlasting.

From this creed we can synthesize a structure of belief that all Christians have in common. They believe

> In God, Creator of things visible and invisible; He is; and he manifests Himself in all reality.
>
> That Jesus is the Messiah, the Christ, Son of God (whether symbolically or literally interpreted).
>
> In the Trinity: the Father, the Son, and the Holy Ghost.
>
> That man is born a sinner and in need of redemption and salvation.
>
> That Jesus Christ came down to earth for the salvation of mankind.
>
> That man has an immortal soul, accountable to God.
>
> That the Bible (both Old and New Testaments) is the accepted guide to follow.
>
> In the historicity of the Gospels.
>
> In the repentance of sinners.
>
> In the life hereafter.
>
> That those who follow Jesus Christ and who repent of their sins will enter the Kingdom of Heaven.

This doctrine makes three key assumptions: (1) man is born a sinner and stands in need of redemption; (2) Jesus Christ came down to earth for the salvation of mankind; and (3) those who follow Jesus Christ (that is, believe in his divine mission) and who repent their sins will enter the Kingdom of Heaven. The implication of these assumptions is that those who do not accept them will continue as sinners, will not enter the Kingdom of Heaven, and will be consigned to eternal punishment.

While promising a vicarious salvation through belief in a

sacrificial savior, it retains the ancient fear of punishment for any failure to "keep the faith." Finally, it contends that earthly existence is important only as a testing ground, a preparation for an unearthly eternity of bliss or punishment in accordance with belief or disbelief in Christian dogma. Its message is clear: "Man is born a sinner and in need of redemption and salvation. . . . Jesus Christ came down to earth for the salvation of mankind. . . . Only those who believe and repent will enter the Kingdom of Heaven."

In other words, the Christian is taught that there is no escape from inborn sinfulness and eternal damnation other than through belief in a savior who will then intercede on his behalf with a vindictive God. Thus the believer is assured that the sins he was born with are forgiven, and he will enjoy eternal reward in an afterlife. There is no other way to be saved; living a blameless life is futile for all men are tainted by the circumstance of birth. Salvation must come through faith alone, according to Christian dogma.

We are left with the only logical conclusion: Christianity is founded on fear—the fear of sin and its consequences—and on a faith that believers will be rewarded with eternal bliss. The purpose and meaning of life for its adherents, then, is avoidance of the stick and pursuit of the carrot, which represent the recompense in some vague afterlife concocted by the Christian priesthood.

This concept of life's purpose is one of the weakest links in the chain of Christian dogma and leads the thinkers among us to wonder how anyone could remain satisfied for long with such a premise.

If such a structure of fear and faith, stick and carrot provides a viable religious edifice, it is difficult to discover how it has brought about any appreciable improvement in the human condition in the past 2,000 years. In that period of time the Holy Wars, Crusades, inquisitions, worldwide internecine conflicts, rampant crime and violence, and a corrupt social order bear witness to the fact that the conduct of mankind, viewed as a collective entity, has failed to improve under the influence of Christianity.

Some of the more perceptive among us have long held the view that Christianity has obstructed spiritual and scientific progress for centuries. The late Bertrand Russell, distinguished freethinker, contended that not only has Christianity failed to improve the lot of man, it has managed to make things worse. Writing in *Why I Am Not a Christian,* he declared that the more intense the religion of any period and the more profound the dogmatic belief, the greater the cruelty and the worse the state of affairs. He believed that science can teach us, and our own hearts can teach us no longer to look around for imaginary supports, no longer to invent allies in the sky, but rather to look to our own efforts here below to make this world a fit place in which to live, instead of the sort of place the churches in all these centuries have made it.

More recently, the civil war between Christians and Moslems has brought widespread death and destruction to the unfortunate country of Lebanon. And in Northern Ireland, Christians continue to slaughter one another and innocent bystanders in the conflict between Protestant and Catholic factions.

With this kind of track record extending back to its very beginnings, it is understandable why Christianity has been branded the most bloodthirsty religion ever devised by man. It would doubtless impress the space traveler from a highly developed society as the product of a race still caught up in a curious form of savagery. With the sanguinary cruelty of a crucifixion as its *raison d'être,* bloodshed, torture, and death became its stock in trade. Without the barbarity of human sacrifice and the symbolism of the cross, its theological trumpets would be muted. Without the pervasive idea of blood—"the blood of the lamb [Christ] taketh away the sins of the world"—its aggressive evangelism would be blunted. Its preoccupation with blood even carries over into the symbolic cannibalism of the ritual of Holy Communion where the wine drunk and the bread eaten represent the blood and body of Christ.

It should also be pointed out that Christian orthodoxy has consistently opposed the diminution of human ignorance and the relief of human suffering. The Inquisition was not only the instrument of cruelty, as noted by Russell, but of a mindless censorship as well. It managed to silence the voice of inquiry in Italy, the birthplace of the Renaissance, for centuries. As one example, Galileo, who supported the Copernican theory that the earth moves around the sun, was denounced as a heretic and imprisoned by the Catholic Church. A more recent example of this kind of bigotry is the ban on birth control by Catholicism in an overpopulated world, an attitude that can only multiply human misery in the years to come.

As we have seen, Christianity by its own tenets offers no purpose for this life other than as preparation for a future state of existence in which the soul will get its just deserts— either eternal punishment or eternal bliss. The former is portrayed as the familiar fire and brimstone of hell; the latter as an unending condition devoted to praising and glorifying a God whose appetite for adulation is apparently insatiable.

Let us digress here and take a closer look at this Christian

God, for the true measure of any religion can be found in the kind of God it worships. We are immediately struck by the fact that in its literature and ministry the Church is so involved with Jesus Christ that God the Father often comes on in a supportive role. For example, in the fourteen items of the Apostles' Creed, cited earlier, God is mentioned only twice while eight statements refer to Christ. Although the amorphous presence of the Father is usually implied or assumed, the Christian is never left in doubt concerning the real star of the canonical drama—Jesus Christ, the Savior, the Son of God.

What does the Christian really believe about this shadowy figure all but eclipsed by the brilliance of the Son? There is no simple, straightforward answer. It is necessary to reconcile the lip service paid to a stylized supreme and perfect being with the Scriptures (the "accepted guide") and with professed beliefs—an involutional task.

From the synthesis of the Apostles' Creed we determined that God is seen as the Creator of things visible and invisible; He is, and He manifests Himself in all reality. The Church catechism contains this statement: "God is a spirit, infinite, eternal, and unchangeable in His being, wisdom, power, holiness, justice, goodness, and truth." And Alexander Cruden gave this description of the Christian God: "This is one of the names which we give to that eternal, infinite, and incomprehensible being, the creator of all things, who preserves and governs everything by His almighty power and wisdom, and who is the only object of our worship."

Obviously Cruden, a Scottish biblical compiler of the eighteenth century, reached the conclusion that "God is the only object of our worship" before the deification of Christ achieved its present magnitude. In this regard one is moved to admiration for the more balanced Jewish belief that denies the divinity of Christ while according him the status of a great teacher.

Be that as it may, we must continue in our efforts to identify the kind of supreme being the Christian projects through the prism of his beliefs. The concept entering this prism is that of an infinite being who created everything that is, who is the complete master of his creation, and whose attributes include every imaginable perfection. Furthermore, such a being is seen as omnipotent, omniscient, and omnipresent.

But the image emerging from the belief-prism has suffered distortions that diminish the original all-powerful, all-loving Father to that of a fickle deity displaying some of the less admirable human traits, including a degree of childish petulance.

The Christian idea of original sin—that man is born a sinner and stands in need of redemption—brings the image of a capricious God into sharper focus. It also constitutes the major difference between this theology and other belief systems. Judaism, for example, teaches that man is born innocent and remains so as long as he conquers his evil impulses. Vastly more followers have been attracted to Christianity because it allows the sinner to be "saved" by a surrogate merely through a profession of faith. On the other hand, Judaism requires the individual to assume responsibility for his own destiny, thus eliminating the need for a sacrificial scapegoat—the be-all and end-all of Christendom. Essentially cynical and pessimistic in its view of man, Christianity denies that humanity is capable of improving its condition by its own efforts.

The presumption of original sin also denies the perfect

justice of an immutable God. The inconsistency of preordained iniquity in the presumably perfect creation of a responsible, compassionate, and presumably perfect Father-God is inescapable. And such incongruities have been intolerable to those unhampered by Christian delusions. Omar Khayyam, that perceptive poet-philosopher of the twelfth century, expressed his own misgivings in this quatrain:

> *Oh, Thou who didst with pitfall and with gin*
> *Beset the road I was to wander in,*
> *Thou wilt not with predestined evil round*
> *Enmesh my soul, and then impute my fall to sin!*

This is the deity who gave man free will but condemned Adam and his posterity forever because of a misadventure in the Garden of Eden—although such an event had to be foreordained in his omniscience. This is the deity who, frustrated by his own handiwork, "repented that he had made man" and sought to rectify matters by bringing a global flood upon his creation, destroying "all flesh that moved upon the earth" with the exception of the family of Noah and other air-breathing life forms which could be accommodated in the ark.

It might be interesting at this point to deal more fully with the Deluge and Noah's Ark, the most dramatic event in the Old Testament, but such a study is irrelevant to our present purpose. Furthermore, any elaboration would only serve to accentuate the ruthlessness of the Christian God, not to mention the absurdities inherent in the Noah tale. Yet the believer is not only undaunted by this unflattering portrayal of his deity, but he bends every effort to validate the biblical recital. Indeed, there is archaeological evidence of a devastating flood some six thousand years ago, but it does not necessarily follow that a punitive god unleashed it or that somebody in a boat salvaged the representatives of every air-breathing species on earth. Yet a number of popular books by Christian writers seeks to prove that remains of the ark can be found on Mount Ararat and, conversely, that the God of Genesis is still the object of Christian worship.

It was this God of Genesis who, upon realizing that his Flood was an exercise in futility and after pondering the problem of human iniquity for additional millennia, came up with the ultimate answer. It was a solution that spawned a new religion which over the past 2,000 years has generated countless spoken and written words attempting to explain and justify it. This solution involved sending his "only-begotten" son to earth to be sacrificed on the altar of man's sinfulness. This barbaric event was intended to dramatize the premise that the *only way* a species born in sin could be redeemed was by the crucifixion of a blameless man-god. In other words, God became the agency of filicide so that man might sin with impunity. Those who believed in this proposition and repented their sins would be rewarded in the next life; those who did not believe and repent would remain under condemnation and suffer in the hereafter.

It is noteworthy that no divine concern is shown for the prevention and cure of sin itself—a congenital and devastating malady pandemic in the human race since the "fall" of Adam. Even the limited human intellect can recognize this as a more rational approach to the problem.

Jesus recognized the efficacy of such an approach and proclaimed throughout his ministry on various levels of understanding that man has the power within his own consciousness to transform his experienced reality. Such a transformation would bring him a more abundant life and a world without sin. In the 2,000 years since this Spiritual Proclamation was issued few humans have understood it or acted upon it. If there had been a general acceptance of this radical concept, the Christian conglomerate as it now exists would be out of business and all the clergy, including the Pope, would be among the unemployed. But this is a remote possibility, for too many people have a vested interest in the status quo and are prepared to go to any extremes to preserve it.

It should also be noted that the Christian equates sin with any infraction of the Mosaic Law capsulized in the Ten Commandments. The second commandment of this moral code explicitly prohibits the use of any kind of image in religious devotions: "Thou shalt not make unto thee any graven image, or any likeness of *anything* that is in heaven above, or that is in the earth beneath, or that is in the water under the earth." Ironically, Christianity is guilty of this "sin" on a monumental scale with its graven images and likenesses of Jesus Christ, the Virgin Mary, and numerous man-made saints which are displayed and venerated throughout Christendom.

Furthermore, the ubiquitous cross is idolized wherever the faithful gather. They even wear crucifixes around their necks and ritually cross themselves in the conviction that such things will conjure up divine indulgence and favoritism. But the one man responsible for this universal symbol is largely ignored by the Church. Had it not been for Judas Iscariot, the betrayer of Christ, there would have been no cross, no crucifixion, no resurrection, and no Christian religion. Never has any theology owed so much to the perfidy of one individual. If it were completely honest, the Church would accord Judas the veneration reserved for its saints, who became saints only as a result of his duplicity.

Physician, heal thyself.

3

Unorthodox Constructions

The race of men, while sheep in credulity, are wolves for conformity.—Carl Van Doren

It has been said that almost anything can be proved by the Bible, that it is subject to many different interpretations. How could it be otherwise? The Bible was written over a 1,400-year period by many different men, most of them unidentified. Its authors were communicating with a diversity of people at different times, under different circumstances, and for a variety of purposes. Inevitably the material was colored by each writer's personality and level of understanding. In addition, the first Council of Nicaea (A.D. 325) and subsequent councils arbitrarily drew up a list of books to be retained in the "inspired" Bible and deleted others. Thus, the Holy Bible, the "accepted guide," is the product of selectivity and censorship applied to the voluminous writings available to the Old and New Testament compilers.

It is to be expected that such a hodgepodge would be riddled with repetitions and inconsistencies. Still, it is a valid assumption that the biblical writers were rational men, that they were depicting reality in the light of their own understanding. Yet rational men are subject to the ignorance, superstitions, and cultural mores of their times, and their narratives would reflect these aberrations.

In the Old Testament stories it was commonplace for a partisan God to become personally involved in the mundane affairs of men and to make special dispensations on behalf of a favored group. With their proclivity for worshiping whatever they did not understand, the ancients could be expected to view inexplicable phenomena as the activities of a godlike being. But what was really going on here? Was it something entirely different from anything a literal-minded reader might discover? And in the most dramatic events of the New Testament—the virgin birth, the miracles, crucifixion, and resurrection of Christ—is there more to be found here than a warmed-over version of pagan doctrines and its adoption by Christian zealots? This particular question, which is crucial to any critique of Christianity, will be dealt with in Part Two.

In all of this one thing is certain: scriptural validities will hardly be recognized by the Fundamentalist. Such discoveries are more likely reserved for those more dispassionate and flexible seekers determined to extract the truth as it was filtered through the mentalities of antiquity.

Such efforts can open up new vistas of thought and conjecture, leading to some startling conclusions. From this perspective we can view the man Jesus and his teachings in a new light. We can draw valid deductions that are at variance with orthodox beliefs. We may even find a stronger rationale supporting the inference that Christ was a missionary from some super race than there is for a belief in his divinity.

The percepts espoused by Jesus have been traditionally construed as repentance and atonement for sin—for "man is born a sinner and in need of redemption and salvation." But the evincible substance of his message in metaphor and parable is concerned with the malady itself; for sin, in essence, is seen to be the result of erroneous thinking and the misapplication of universal laws. This being so, the eradication of sin is as simple and as difficult as changing the patterns of thought.

"Except a man be born again," said the Nazarene, "he cannot see the Kingdom of God." Without a mental and psychic rebirth, man cannot experience a moral reality. But, said the mystic, in Mark 9:23, "If thou canst believe, all things are possible to him that believeth [in the possibility]." As noted earlier, his use of the phrase "the Kingdom of God is within you" is a metaphorical reference to the creative power inherent in human consciousness, which is a non-material component of the Infinite Mind. That man can use this power to transform his experienced reality is the possibility in which he should believe. This is the "good news" buried in the Gospels.

That man is endowed with the equipment and capacity to create and control his own reality is the essence of Genesis if that enigmatic book is given a cabalistic interpretation. When he made his appearance in this milieu man was admonished in Genesis 1:28 to "replenish the earth, and subdue it: and have dominion over the fish of the sea, and over the fowl of the air, and over every living thing that moveth upon the earth." In this context the Earth is the biblical term for experienced reality. With his endowment for dominion over the fish of the sea, the fowl of the air and everything that moves, man is assured he can control his total reality, not just certain aspects of it.

But Adam (a collective term for early man) used his free will to misdirect this creative energy toward hylotheistic, self-serving goals. The "fall of man" constituted a mental/psychic lapse rather than a physical one as the Christian notion of original sin would have it. At that time mankind abdicated its rightful place in the Kingdom of Consciousness (the "Garden of Eden") as its highest expression of creative intelligence and exchanged its birthright for a mess of hedonistic pottage. With its heritage of mental/psychic indolence, the species has found itself earthbound and committed to a self-defeating reality of its own making.

The mystic mind of Jesus encompassed the origins and course of the human experience, and the thrust of his message was an effort to awaken the sleepwalker to a realization of his latent creative powers. His mission was not concerned with vicarious salvation but with a revival of the creative intelligence previously disowned—a reminder that man could "come to himself" and recover his birthright.

Jesus' Parable of the Prodigal Son is a concise chronicle of the human predicament expressed in contemporary terms. The prodigal son (materialistic man) took his inheritance (his rightful place in the Kingdom of Consciousness) into a far country (a denial of his creative powers) and wasted his substance in riotous living (materialism). When at last he came to himself (realized the potentials within his own consciousness), he returned home (to the source within) and reclaimed his true place in the kingdom. The brother who never left home represents that small spiritually enlightened segment of humanity that has been all but overwhelmed by the perversions of the majority. The moral of this story is the assurance that mankind can choose to return to its proper place in the scheme of things. In the parable there is music and dancing in the house upon the prodigal's return (all creation will rejoice if and when man finally comes to himself).

However, according to Christian doctrine, divine interest is confined to the ostensible functions of repentance and professed belief in a Son who will somehow prevail upon a misanthropic God, the instigator of the condition, to deliver the repenters and believers from the consequences of their sinfulness. This is a throwback to the inept God of Genesis, to the primitive doctrine of blood sacrifices for the remission of sin, and to the transference of righteousness from the innocent to the guilty via a suitable scapegoat.

This is the measure of the God of Christianity according to its Bible (the "accepted guide"), its traditions, and beliefs. And it becomes increasingly clear why the Christian wholeheartedly embraces the Son while relegating the Father, the callous despot, to a subordinate role. With this kind of deity, it is not surprising that the Christian views earthly existence as a never-never land whose principal significance lies in its function as a foreordained sin trap from which the individual can extricate himself only by the abdication of reason and a blind reliance on a sacrificial savior.

This is the faith of our fathers, the old-time religion. " 'Tis the old-time religion and it's good enough for me," runs an old hymn. This is the theme song of millions of modern Christians who have renounced their intellectual faculties and followed a will-o'-the-wisp into the cul-de-sac of a vicarious atonement. This is the easy way of mental indolence, an affliction almost as pandemic in the human race as sin itself. It provides a crutch and a cop-out for the multitudes who are only too glad to shirk personal responsibility for their destiny.

As a religion which has traditionally opposed independent thought as heretical, Christianity has sapped the spiritual growth of untold numbers. In all times the organized Church has extolled the unthinking follower while condemning those who march to a different drummer. It thrives on the herd instincts of credulity and conformity. As Charlotte Perkins Gilman expressed it, "To swallow and follow, whether old doctrine or new propaganda, is a weakness still dominating the human mind."

In this book we are attempting to throw off the shackles of primitive fear, of unquestioning faith, and of misguided orthodoxy, for together they are as irrational as the pagan beginnings of all religion—which we smugly feel we have somehow outgrown. Let us assert with Sir Arthur Keith: "No creed is final; such a creed as mine must grow and change as knowledge grows and changes."

Let us recognize fear and faith for what they are: stepping-stones to reason. Without reason and her handmaidens, imagination and intuition, we are destined to swallow and follow forever. On the basis of fear and faith those of us concerned with the hypostasis of religion in general and of Christianity in particular have found ourselves on a circular course. We have felt as did Omar Khayyam when he wrote in the *Rubaiyat:*

> *Myself when young did eagerly frequent*
> *Doctor and saint, and heard great argument*
> *About it and about; but evermore*
> *Came out by the same door wherein I went.*

We can overcome the irrationalities of fear and faith that have dominated our species to its detriment for so long and declare with Daniel Webster: "Mind is the great lever of all things; human thought is the process by which human needs are answered." This is not to say that faith, per se, is the irrational counterpart of primitive fear. It becomes unreliable and fatuous only when it usurps the power of thought. And it is this kind of faith that sustains the intrinsic delusions of Christianity.

It would appear that such a religion as Christianity is necessary until people outgrow it or in some way attain to a level of consciousness that recognizes the trappings of self-delusion—whether it takes two thousand years or five thousand. In any event, the time will come when the gods of today will be as forgotten as those of a buried continent and, unless man grows up, others will be worshiped and each of them will claim to be the creator of the world and of man. And other Sons of God will supersede Jesus as Jesus supplanted earlier man-gods with such names as Bel-Merodach, Osiris, Mithras. Such a belief system can undergo repetitive deaths and resurrections until the end of time unless man resolves to get off his religious merry-go-round and assume responsibility for his own destiny.

We will employ reason and her handmaidens in submitting that Jesus was not the divinity exploited by Christianity; neither was he indigenous to this planet; and, further, that his teachings have been grossly misinterpreted. This was recognized by the Master himself when he said, "Those who are with me have not understood me."

We will be mindful that his death and resurrection—the lifeblood of Christian theology—were described by ingenuous gospel writers remote in time and place from the actual events and dependent in large measure upon suspect information from a small clique with a religious ax to grind. Moreover, the temptation to embellish upon incidents crucial to an infant religion could well have been irresistible to those zealous advocates.

For those who are not overawed by the canonical narratives the incredible truth is suggested by an eyewitness account in the New Testament Apocrypha. An imaginative interpretation of this and other arcane material will open up byways of exploration and discovery impugned by the organized Church.

While Jesus did not embody perfection (the Gospels themselves bear witness to his foibles), we contend that he was a metaphysical genius with a profound message for all mankind. It is true he was not of this world, as the equivocal New Testament sources imply, but they were wide of the mark in describing him as a Divine Emissary. We submit that such an exceptional figure could have no connection, filial or otherwise, with the kind of God depicted by Christian tradition.

Nor was the principal burden of his message an admonition to prepare for the life to come, as Christian doctrine maintains. This is refuted in his own words, as reported in John 10:10: ". . . I am come that they might have life, and that they might have it more abundantly." A realistic interpretation of his teachings will reveal that he was formulating the requisites for a do-it-yourself salvation. Jesus was prescribing the antidote and cure for a sin-sick society. He was laying out the blueprint for a better world in the here and now—a world whose determinants originate on the mental plane.

4

An Earth-Centered Theology

*If a thousand old beliefs were ruined in our march
to truth, we must still march on.—Stopford A. Brooke*

Emerson once said, "Science corrects the old creeds,
sweeps away with every new perception our infantile catechism, and necessitates a faith commensurate with the grander
orbits and universal laws which it discloses." One can only
wish this were a truism vis-à-vis Christianity and the science
of astronomy, which has discovered billions of other worlds
in the vastness of space.

When one looks into the matter, he is astounded at the
lag between the march of knowledge and its acceptance by

organized religion. More than a century before Galileo, the astronomical studies of the "Universal Genius" Leonardo da Vinci (1452-1519) produced the idea that the sun does not move. He had begun to displace man from the center of the universe. In the 1600s Galileo confirmed the theories of da Vinci and Copernicus which refuted the teachings of the Church that everything revolved around man and his tiny planet. As previously noted, Galileo was denounced by the Inquisition and imprisoned, and scientific progress was hamstrung for generations.

Four hundred years later the accumulation of irrefutable evidence has compelled the Christian priesthood to recant and it now concedes that, indeed, the earth does move around the sun. But that is the only concession it has been willing to make to the grander orbits revealed by science. With the heritage of an Inquisition, it is still convinced that a barbarous race inhabiting a cosmic speck on the fringes of a commonplace galaxy is the darling of all creation. This race is so favored, in fact, that a partisan deity, for some obscure reason, abrogates the universal principles of physical reality for its sole benefit. Many such instances are recounted in the Bible, the "accepted guide." One that immediately comes to mind is divine intervention attending the exodus of the Children of Israel from Egypt. Another is the resurrection of Christ from the dead after his crucifixion.

But such a deity is not always beneficent. He has been credited with drowning a world in an attempt to destroy the wicked; then attempting to "save" the survivors' posterity by sacrificing an anomalistic son for his own appeasement. The word attempt is used advisedly for it is obvious that neither the Deluge nor the crucifixion of Christ has had any salutary effect on the human condition.

To put the most charitable light on the matter, this God concept envisions a creator who is neither supreme in his creation nor consistent in his treatment of it. Perhaps this God is learning from experience and evolving like the rest of us. If this is the case, we can only hope he is evolving at a more rapid rate than the species made in his image and after his likeness. Still, it is interesting to speculate on a God who learns from divine mistakes, as this affords the only rational explanation for the Christian God of Scripture. Certainly the God of the New Testament is a great improvement over the deity of the Old Testament. The latter could devise no remedy for human iniquity other than near-total annihilation of the race; whereas the former has advanced to the novel concept of murdering only one man—his own son—for the remission of sins. It must be admitted that the scheme of using a sacrificial savior has much to commend it in terms of economy in human lives and efficiency of execution.

Six thousand years after the Flood and 2,000 years after the crucifixion of Christ—two widely separated and ineffective efforts to reform mankind—there are signs and portents that an evolving God is considering yet another solution to the human enigma. From all indications he is fed up with this particular experiment and would like to wash his hands of the whole business. It was nothing less than a stroke of genius to provide a childish race with the lethal toys that could one day consume it in a nuclear holocaust. This may be the ultimate in poetic justice.

According to cosmologists, our solar system is a Johnny-come-lately in the macrocosm. There were many billions of star systems and uncountable planets before we were even a gleam in the Father's eye. How many other worlds and how many other races did the Christian God have to deal with before Homo sapiens put in a belated appearance? If these were Divine experiments commensurate with the scriptural accounts of creation and its aftermath, we are faced with inferences that defy all reason. Have there been innumerable Adams, Gardens of Eden, Floods, Noahs, Christs, crucifixions, resurrections? How many "only-begotten" sons can any one God have? How many extraterrestrial races have been "saved" by a man-god scapegoat only to sentence themselves to nuclear extinction?

Christianity is discomfited by such questions, for it always has been, and for its own survival must continue to be, a provincial theology. Just as it resisted the idea of a solar system, a galaxy, that does not revolve around man, it resists the idea that man is not the only intelligent being in the cosmos. It still nurtures a belief in a mechanical universe and a provincial God whose chief, if not only, concern is Man and his antics in this kindergarten of galactic civilization.

This earth-centered doctrine may one day be called upon to resist the most heretical idea of all: that a God who is capable of creating one universe, the one we know, could create any number of other universes in any number of dimensions. A being responsible for the spectrum of light could also envisage a spectrum of cosmic systems. Who can establish the creative limits of Infinite Intelligence?

A more immediate threat to this provincial doctrine has been knocking at its portals with mounting insistence for many years—the UFO phenomenon. Unearthly devices of the UFO genre and their crews have been recorded in the myths and legends, artifacts, cave paintings and rock drawings of ancient cultures around the world. The Old Testament itself (the "accepted guide") is replete with references to mysterious beings with awesome powers who intervened in the affairs of men. One explicit example is the celestial machine reported by the prophet Ezekiel which he described as "a wheel in the middle of a wheel." This disk-shaped spinning craft with the hard, lustrous appearance of beryl "lifted up" the prophet and transported him to "the east gate of the Lord's house."

In the past several decades increased UFO activity with many reported occupant-human contacts could presage a confrontation sooner or later with an out-of-this-world race of humanoid beings. They may be so superior to Homo sapiens in intellectual and psychic development that the nature and concepts of such a society will be as incomprehensible to modern man as they were to the celestial-minded cultures of the Old Testament. When that eventuality occurs, provincial religious beliefs will suffer the same fate as all the other homemade delusions of an inchoate civilization.

Christian doctrine, as it has been spelled out and proselytized, confronts the rationalist with unconscionable absurdities. Still, he must take care not to throw out the baby with the bath water. For the possibility remains that an infant of truth may be lurking in the murky waters of dogma.

5

Religions Are Man-Made

If God did not exist it would be necessary to invent him.—Voltaire

All religions have two things in common which, paradoxically, are mutually exclusive. Each claims to be an infallible guide on the path to heaven (whatever and wherever that may be) yet all are the inventions of fallible human minds. If there is any truth in the axiom that like begets like, then it is obviously absurd to expect oranges from lemon trees, good results from evil deeds, or ultimate truth from finite mentalities.

Yet such intellects have taken a perverse delight in fabricating one belief system after another which through the ages have led trusting humankind down many a primrose path. Religious inventiveness reached a peak in the fourteen centuries between 700 B.C. to about A.D. 700, when nearly all the sacred books of all the great religions were created, assembled, and canonized. Why this particular period in human history supplied such fertile soil for religious movements is a matter of conjecture and should provide an interesting field for further research.

A major religion of this period was established in ancient Persia (now Iran) in the seventh century B.C. by a self-styled prophet, Zarathustra, whom the Greeks called Zoroaster. Curiosity and interest in this religion existed in the centuries immediately preceding and immediately following the birth of Christ.

The purpose of its founder seems to have been to reform the religion of his people, probably because it was excessively priest-ridden and demanded animal sacrifices its agricultural economy could ill afford. Zoroaster believed in a good and wise God who created all things, a devil, a heaven, and a hell. The struggle between God and devil convulses the world, but God will triumph in the end, and there will be a last judgment in which the devil and all who serve him will finally be punished.

In becoming the faith of the Mesopotamian peoples, Zoroastrianism underwent significant changes. After his death Zoroaster was transfigured into a magical personage whose birth was attended by a miracle. His representative, the Saoshyant, a messianic figure (the first in history), was to come at the end of earthly time and reign over humanity before the last judgment.

Needless to say, this ancient doctrine has curious similarities to the belief system inspired by Jesus Christ seven centuries later.

Half a world away and in a much later time frame Pacific island natives were inspired to invent a new religion of their own. The source of their inspiration was the sudden appearance of thundering chariots from the heavens shaped like crosses and belching fire and smoke. From these awesome sky craft emerged white godlike beings who spoke a strange language and carried magic sticks whose noise brought down distant game. They introduced the tribe to the delights of fire cookery, the benefits of agriculture and house building, and the healing miracles of modern medicine.

But one day the white gods climbed into their flying crosses, roared down the hard, smooth pathways they had built, and disappeared into the heavens from whence they had come.

When their benefactors failed to return within a reasonable time, the tribal elders decreed that replicas of the chariots should be constructed as objects of worship and that nightly fires should be lit on the smooth pathways as guiding beacons. As time passed this ritual became a tradition whose origins were glorified in song and story. The mystique of the white sky gods and their beneficent influence became the doctrine of a tribal religion symbolized by a cross.

When members of the U.S. bomber squadron who had occupied a remote island in the Pacific during the war against Japan were informed of their deification by the natives, they were amused. But the squadron commander took a more serious view of the matter. Said he, "I suppose no harm will come from it unless they take it upon themselves to convert their heathen neighbors. History is replete with the evils attendant upon missionary zeal." He shuddered. "I certainly would not want anything like that on my conscience."

According to latest reports, the islanders have not yet succumbed to compulsive evangelism, which characterizes a number of religious movements, with Christianity being the most aggressive of all time. But these simple natives still religiously set nightly signal fires to facilitate the Second Coming.

6

Mohammed and Christ

A man may be a heretic in the truth; and if he believes things only on the authority of others without other reason, then, though his belief be true, yet the very truth he holds becomes heresy.—Milton

The nearest rival to Christianity in terms of converts is Islam with over half a billion followers. A mixture of Jewish and Christian beliefs, this faith originated in the Arabian city of Mecca with the birth of Mohammed into an aristocratic family of the Koreish tribe about A.D. 570.

After his death, legends arose about the many miracles accompanying Mohammed's birth. The stars sang in praise of Allah (God), and mountains and valleys responded, lauding the newborn child. Temples crumbled in faroff countries. And in distant Persia in the temples of Zoroaster the Eternal Fire, which had burned steadily for centuries, went out. The earth quaked with joy and idols all over the world tumbled down from their pedestals. And everywhere the omens foretold that a great and godly manchild had been born to cleanse the earth of idolatry and corruption.

At the age of twenty Mohammed became the caravan guide and steward of a wealthy and attractive middle-aged widow, Khadijah, whom he eventually married. He became a rich and respected merchant of Mecca and would doubtless have lived out his life unknown to either history or religion had he not begun to have dreams and visions during meditation. In these dreams he was told by the angel Gabriel that he, Mohammed, was Allah's messenger and should read the divine revelations and write them down. As Mohammed was uneducated and could neither read nor write, he obtained the services of a learned scribe to record his visions. Mohammed called this record "The Reading" because the angel Gabriel had commanded him to read.

In the early years of his ministry Mohammed learned of a plot against his life among the merchants and leaders of Mecca and fled the city on the night of June 20, A.D. 622. This date became the most memorable in Islam, the religion founded by Mohammed. It is called the Night of the Flight. Just as the Jews count the years from the Week of Creation, and Christians count the years from the birth of Christ, so Mohammedans or Moslems (True Believers) count time from the Year of the Flight (anno Hegira or A.H.).

After Mohammed's death at the age of sixty-two, his visions, speeches, and sermons were collected into a book called the Koran, which means "The Reading." To the

Moslems every word in the Koran is the actual Word of God as revealed to Mohammed by the angel Gabriel in dreams. It can be said that Islam, one of the world's great religions, is founded on dreams—an adaptation of the dreamworld crucial to the beginnings of Christianity, its predecessor.

Dreams played an important role during the Advent of Jesus Christ as recorded in the canonical Gospels. An angel of the Lord appeared to Joseph in a dream and admonished him to accept the pregnancy of Mary, his virgin wife, as the issue of the Holy Ghost. The Wise Men from the East come to worship the Holy Child were warned by God in a dream that they should not return to Herod (who plotted to kill the future Savior) but should go back to their own country by another way. Joseph was again visited by an angel of the Lord in a dream. This time he was advised to flee with the child Jesus into Egypt for Herod sought to destroy him. Later more dreams guided the Holy Family back to Israel.

An uneducated Mohammed was unable to make a personal record of his teachings, but he did have the foresight to enlist the services of a trusted and learned scribe who was solely responsible for preserving the revelations of the Master in written form. On the other hand, we are led by the Gospel accounts to conclude that Jesus was an educated man. At the age of twelve, according to Luke, Jesus was found sitting in the Temple at Jerusalem amidst the doctors, both hearing them and asking them questions. "And all that heard him were astonished at his understanding and answers." Again we are told in Luke that after his baptism by John some eighteen years later Jesus stood up to *read* in the synagogue and "all wondered at the gracious words which proceeded from his mouth."

If Jesus could read, it is reasonable to assume he could

also write. Why, then, did he put nothing in writing concerning his ministry and do nothing to preserve the precise meaning of his teachings? It would appear that a prudent man would take whatever steps were necessary to safeguard a message of such profound importance to all mankind. While Mohammed, who must have known of the weaknesses of Christianity, avoided ambiguity and misinterpretation by designating a single individual to record his sermons and dreams, Jesus entrusted his oral teachings to the frailties of human recollection many years after his voice had been silenced.*

At this point several avenues of conjecture are open to us. We can acknowledge the Christian deification of Christ and the corollary that he shared the godly attribute of omniscience. Indeed there is a report in Matthew that Jesus foretold his betrayal and crucifixion. And in several other Gospel accounts he is represented as predicting conflict and unrest in the practice of his principles. Considering the radical nature of his message, such a prediction could have been made by anyone familiar with it. However, it is clear that no one, including Jesus, could foresee that his simple teachings would develop into a doctrinal monstrosity plagued by controversy, persecution, cruelty, and bloodshed—instigated by proponents and opponents alike.

If, then, Jesus lacked the attributes of Divinity, as that term is understood and employed by Christian theologians,

---

*In St. John's Revelation he is commanded by Jesus to write down certain things to be delivered to the seven churches in Asia. However, since Jesus was dead at the time and John admits that he himself was "in the spirit," this hardly qualifies as a person-to-person record á la Mohammed. Furthermore, this final book of the Scriptures is essentially a vehicle for the obscure rantings of a writer who is obviously demented.

was he a mortal like Mohammed? An affirmative answer to that question is qualified by the realization that an uneducated man like Mohammed still had the acumen to record his teachings while Jesus did not.

This opens up a third and final avenue of speculation. We can assume that Jesus put nothing in writing because he overestimated the abilities of Homo sapiens and misjudged its capacity for faithful retention of the spoken word and the exact nature of past events. What kind of being would make such a faulty assessment? Could an extraordinary personage such as Jesus—versed in the law, reader in the synagogue, wise counselor, teacher, and miracle worker—make such a mistake? An affirmative answer is unavoidable for no Christian equivalent of the Koran was ever compiled.

This line of reasoning leads to an inference which at first glance may appear to exceed the bounds of credibility. But it is in actuality no more incredible than the mixture of supernatural and miraculous events every Christian is required to accept on faith. He is expected to believe that Christ came from the union of a virgin with an angel or some kind of ghost; that he became flesh and allowed himself to be crucified as the only way a sinful humanity could be saved from perdition; that after his crucifixion he descended into hell and "on the third day arose from the dead, ascended into heaven and sitteth on the right hand of God the Father." And what could be more incredible than the circumstances surrounding the Passion as described by Matthew?

In the twenty-seventh chapter of this Gospel we read: "Jesus [on the cross] when he had cried again with a loud voice, yielded up the ghost. And, behold, the veil of the temple was rent in twain from the top to the bottom; and the earth did quake, and the rocks rent; and the graves were opened; and many bodies of the saints which slept arose, and came out of the graves after his resurrection, and went into the holy city, and appeared to many."

Not content with the miraculous resurrection of just one man, Jesus, Matthew feels obliged to pile miracle upon miracle by raising a flock of saints from their interment in the local cemetery. One can imagine the consternation, even terror, these walking dead must have occasioned their relatives and friends. But Matthew allows this affair to die a natural death, as well he should. It must have dawned upon him that any further attention given the revived saints would only detract from his main thesis—the resurrection of the Savior. And no self-respecting gospel writer would allow his Redeemer to play second fiddle regardless of the provocation. In passing one is led to wonder why the ecclesiastical censors allowed this reference to revitalized saints to remain in the canonical Gospels.

Such clumsy and transparent efforts to weave an aura of divinity around the person of Jesus lend added credibility to the premise that he was not the so-called only-begotten Son of God nor even an exceptional member of Homo sapiens. Lateral thinking* brings us to the conclusion that he had to be an emissary from a highly developed other-world race in which eidetic memory is commonplace and thus taken for granted. This being the case, such an entity would not as a matter of course concern himself with written records.

This provides the only rational explanation for what can be termed the dereliction of Jesus in contrast to the prudence

---

*As opposed to vertical thinking, which consists in digging the same hole deeper, lateral thinking is the digging of new holes.

exercised by Mohammed. But much more is needed to establish the Master's transmundane origin and, of equal consequence, the motivation behind such a difficult and dangerous mission. This can be done by using those handmaidens of reason mentioned earlier: imagination and intuition. They can be employed to extrapolate selections from that mass of expunged writings, the Apocryphal Gospels, which can shed startling new light on the Christ phenomenon and contradict 2,000 years of superstitious belief.

PART TWO

From the cowardice that shrinks
from new truth,
From the laziness that is content
with half-truths,
From the arrogance that thinks it
knows all truth,
Oh, God of Truth deliver us.
—Ancient Hebrew Prayer

7

The Infant Prodigy

We must never throw away a bushel of truth because it happens to contain a few grains of chaff; on the contrary, we may sometimes profitably receive a bushel of chaff for the few grains of truth it may contain.—A. P. Stanley

The Holy Bible, as it was compiled and canonized over the centuries, inevitably accumulated huge amounts of chaff. The truth-seeker is obliged to employ great diligence in winnowing the true from the false, in gleaning authentic interpretations from the bushels of misrepresentations, distortions and inaccuracies, plus the many embellishments intended to amplify the appeal of a struggling religion.

The Apocryphal literature, particularly the New Testament Apocrypha, which is even more voluminous than the canonical version, presents the serious investigator with a much more demanding task of evaluation and selectivity. The amount of chaff that must be sifted for a few grains of truth represents a formidable undertaking, and it is understandable why the biblical compilers decided to throw out the whole apocryphal bushel rather than involve themselves in the tedious winnowing process.

Evidence of this procedure is most apparent in the infancy stories of Jesus. There is only one specific reference to his childhood precocity in the canonical Gospels where Luke relates how the twelve-year-old boy was found by his parents in a learned discussion with the doctors in the temple at Jerusalem. In contrast, the extirpated gospels are replete with explicit accounts of the wonders worked by the Holy Infant. Some of these "miracles" were laudable, some the result of childish whims, and others were, to say the least, of a vindictive character.

A few examples from *The Infancy Story of Thomas** will serve to illustrate the tenor of these childhood narratives:

> When this boy Jesus was five years old he was playing at the ford of a brook, and he gathered together into pools the water that flowed by, and made it at once clean, and commanded it by his word alone. He made soft clay and fashioned from it twelve sparrows. And it was the sabbath when he did this. And there were also many other children

---

*From *New Testament Apocrypha*, Volume One, edited by Wilhelm Schneemelcher and Edgar Hennecke. English translation edited by R. McL. Wilson. Published in the U.S.A. by The Westminster Press, 1963. Copyright © 1959 J. C. B. Mohr (Paul Siebeck), Tübingen. English trans-translation © 1963 Lutterworth Press. All footnotes, paragraph, and verse numbers appearing in the original have been omitted. Used by permission.

playing with him. Now when a certain Jew saw what Jesus was doing in his play on the sabbath, he at once went and told his father Joseph: "See, your child is at the brook, and he has taken clay and fashioned twelve birds and has profaned the sabbath." And when Joseph came to the place and saw (it), he cried out to him, saying: "Why do you do on the sabbath what ought not to be done?" But Jesus clapped his hands and cried to the sparrows: "Off with you!" And the sparrows took flight and went away chirping. The Jews were amazed when they saw this, and went away and told their elders what they had seen Jesus do. . . .

After this again he went through the village, and a lad ran and knocked against his shoulder. Jesus was exasperated and said to him: "You shall not go further on your way," and the child immediately fell down and died. But some, who saw what took place, said: "From where does this child spring, since his every word is an accomplished deed?" And the parents of the dead child came to Joseph and blamed him and said: "Since you have such a child, you cannot dwell with us in the village; or else teach him to bless and not to curse. For he is slaying our children. . . ."

After a few days a young man was cleaving wood in a *corner,* and the axe fell and split the sole of his foot, and he bled so much that he was about to die. And when a clamour arose and a concourse of people took place, the child Jesus also ran there, and forced his way through the crowd, and took the injured foot, and it was healed immediately. And he said to the young man: "Arise now, cleave the wood and remember me." And when the crowd saw what had happened, they worshipped the child, saying: "Truly the spirit of God dwells in this child. . . ."

Again, in the time of sowing the child went out with

> his father to sow wheat in their land. And as his father sowed, the child Jesus also sowed one corn of wheat. And when he had reaped it and threshed it, he brought in a hundred measures; and he called all the poor of the village to the threshing-floor and gave them the wheat, and Joseph took the residue of the wheat. He was eight years old when he worked this miracle.

Parenthetically, it may be noted that such tales bear a curious resemblance to those concerning the God of Genesis who alternated between benevolence and ruthlessness. Still the diligent seeker may discover a kernel of truth in this bushel of fabrication. Let us take another look at the source referred to above which was translated from the Greek.

> A teacher named Zacchaeus offered to teach Jesus but was early confounded by the child's comprehensive knowledge of the Greek alphabet. He . . . said to those present: "Woe is me, I am forced into a quandary, wretch that I am: I have brought shame to myself in drawing to myself this child. Take him away, therefore, I beseech you, brother Joseph. I cannot endure the severity of his look, *I cannot make out his speech at all. This child is not earth-born* [emphasis added]; he can tame even fire. Perhaps he was begotten even before the creation of the world. . . . Woe is me, my friend, *he stupefies me . . . I cannot follow his understanding.* [emphasis added] . . . Therefore, I ask you, brother Joseph, take him away to your house. He is something great, a god or an angel or what I should say I do not know . . ."*

In contrast to the mythical character of the first four examples cited from the infancy stories of Thomas the last, which describes the impressions of a reputable teacher, carries

---

*Op. cit.

the ring of truth. The fact that he was a real person, a man of intelligence and perception, and not a figment of Thomas's imagination, is borne out if we accept at face value a reference to this same Zacchaeus in the canonical Gospels.

In the nineteenth chapter of Luke we find these passages, which describe incidents during the ministry of Jesus that occurred more than twenty years after he had been a pupil of Zacchaeus:

"And Jesus entered and passed through Jericho. And, behold there was a man named Zacchaeus, which was chief among the publicans, and he was rich. And he sought to see Jesus who he was; and could not for the press, because he was little of stature. And he ran before and climbed up into a sycamore tree to see him: for he was to pass that way. And when Jesus came to the place he looked up, and saw him, and said unto him, 'Zacchaeus, make haste, and come down; for today I must abide at thy house.' And he made haste and came down, and received him joyfully."

Here we have verification that Jesus and Zacchaeus were already known to each other and apparently shared feelings of friendship and respect in spite of, or perhaps because of, their relationship in the past. This quotation from Luke would appear to substantiate the infancy story of Thomas.

Returning to that story, we are even more inclined to regard it as an aspect of truth. And the expressions of the scholarly and astute Zacchaeus pertaining to the child Jesus assume qualities that are more realistic than fanciful.

However, certain key statements are so extraordinary they defy normal explanations: *"I cannot make out his speech at all. This child is not earth-born; he can tame even fire. . . . He stupefies me."*

Throughout history there have been many child prodigies—in music, the arts, science, mathematics, literature— but there was never any doubt they were all conceived and born on this earth, and none spoke unintelligibly or stupefied his teacher.

It is safe to say that Jesus was no ordinary prodigy on the human scale. His knowledge and abilities were so advanced for his age they inspired awe and even a degree of fear in the hearts of those who knew him. It is understandable that his chroniclers would resort to fiction and the supernatural in their attempts to explain the inexplicable. We have seen that most of the Gospel of Thomas was an exercise in fantasy and that only the teaching episode gives any impression of authenticity.

On the other hand, as we have also seen, the canonical Gospels, with the exception of Luke, give only cursory accounts of the infancy of Jesus, and Mark and John have nothing to say about his entrance into the world. Moreover, Matthew and Luke resort to the supernatural to account for the advent of such a wondrous being upon the earth plane. The "virgin birth" as described in Matthew 1:18-25 and in Luke 1:26-35 has the same fictional character as the childish miracles in the extirpated Apocrypha and can be recognized as an elaborate cover-up for their ignorance of the child's true origin. This was a common stratagem employed by both Old and New Testament writers when dealing with recondite material.

The virgin birth not only incorporates the supernatural but contains within itself a curious anomaly. A child born of a virgin who was "conceived in her by the Holy Ghost" could not claim Joseph, the husband of Mary, as his father and, therefore, had no kinship with Joseph's ancestors. But Matthew begins his Gospel with this statement: "The book of the generation of Jesus Christ, the son of David, the son of Abraham." This ancestry is detailed for the next fifteen verses and in the sixteenth verse we find this: "And Jacob begat Joseph the husband of Mary, of whom was born Jesus, who is called Christ." Then, as previously noted, Matthew goes on to relate how Mary was impregnated by the Holy Ghost who could have had no earthly genealogy to confer upon Jesus as this Gospel writer takes such pains to delineate at the beginning of the chapter.

When we consider the four canonical Gospels, does it not seem strange that two of them—Mark and John—make no reference to the birth of Jesus while Matthew and Luke offer explicit descriptions of the "Immaculate Conception"? But even in the face of an anomalous birth Matthew could recognize that Jesus must have Joseph's ancestry to conform with Jewish custom and to comply with Old Testament prophecies of a Messiah who would come from the House of David.

Such tortuous reasoning only serves to convince the astute reader that the origin of Jesus was a mystery 2,000 years ago and remains unresolved to this day. Zacchaeus could have been nearer the truth than the apologists when he exclaimed, "This child is not earth-born!" He might have been even nearer the truth if he had said, "This child was not conceived on earth!"

In the following pages we will develop a thesis based on the testimony of Zacchaeus to account for the advent of Christ. It is a premise that has no counterpart in the religious concepts of earth. However, in the light of current knowledge and advanced scientific thinking, it is well within the bounds of possibility. It might even be said to have a greater coefficient of plausibility than that provided by the supernaturalism of the orthodox Gospels.

8

The Crack in the Macrocosm

*The universe is not only queerer than we imagine—
it is queerer than we CAN imagine.—J. B. S. Haldane*

If the physical reality we perceive is all that queer, it is
no big step in lateral thinking to postulate a parallel universe
in another dimension inhabited by a long-lived race thousands
of years ahead of us in every facet of development. Although
these beings are subject to the same shortcomings as humankind, many have learned to use nearly 100 percent of their
mental capacities, whereas Homo sapiens has rarely used
more than 10 percent of its potential, which as often as not
has been utilized to its own detriment.

We will call this adjacent system Andor—an acronym
for another dimension of reality—and its inhabitants Andori-

ans. Could such a super race have discovered planet earth and developed an interest in the affairs of men?

Let's eavesdrop on a discussion in progress between Andor's co-leaders, whom we will designate Alpha and Omega—the protégé and his mentor. Language is no barrier, for all thoughts are transmitted telepathically. As the dialogue proceeds, we are surprised that no record is being kept of this top-level meeting and even more surprised to learn that our own earth is the topic under discussion, although they have another name for it—Aquarius. Another oddity soon confronts us: the time frame is remote from what we think of as the present.

ALPHA: It would appear we have a tiger by the tail or, if you prefer, a monkey on our backs.

OMEGA: I prefer the latter metaphor as the Aquarian still exhibits the characteristics of a carnal, superstitious, naked ape forty years after our ill-starred experiment.

ALPHA: Ah, yes, the experiment. That is what put the monkey on our backs. It all began, as I recall, when five of our spacecraft on a training mission encountered a black hole* and were swept into the Aquarian system where they were marooned for centuries. I remember the highlights of this adventure, but I do not find the details in my memory bank.

OMEGA: I can understand such a lapse. You have been

---

*Black holes in space, or cosmic cracks, occur when the nuclear fires of very massive stars are finally extinguished. Their enormous gravity causes them to collapse so completely that they literally squeeze themselves out of existence. Thus a black hole is left in space, and surrounding matter can disappear into this. Such vanishing matter can show up in an adjacent space-time continuum through "white holes." This exchange of matter and/or energy between universes keeps things in balance.

almost exclusively concerned with a resolution of the problem rather than its origins. So I'll give you a brief summary of the Aquarian experience.

To begin with, it is necessary to recognize the time differential. One year of Andorian time is the equivalent of 100 years of Aquarian time. They live much faster and die much sooner. The average Andorian life span of 500 years would thus stretch out to 50,000 years on Aquarius. Therefore, our sojourn on the planet of 240 AQ centuries represents less than half a normal Andorian lifetime. In fact, most members of the marooned fleet were quite young and are still in the prime of life.

Another significant factor is the primitive state in which we found the species. It was an intellectual pygmy and had attained only to a state of simple self-awareness. It was this condition that concerned our highly evolved A-Team and moved them to undertake an experiment designed to develop the psyche and raise the consciousness level of the race. This project was in its early stages when the team was ordered to join the fleet in its search for an interdimensional passageway, or cosmic crack, for the return to Andor.

A lower level group, the D-Team, was left on the planet as a backup for the search mission. This unit attempted to follow through on the A-Team's developmental work. This was most unfortunate, for the D-Team had no conception of the subtleties involved in directing spiritual growth. Being physically oriented themselves, they taught the primitive Aquarians to use mind and energy for the attainment of materialistic rather than psychic goals—the acquisitive versus the creative drive.

ALPHA: Was this the Fall of Man, as it is fancifully described in their religious literature?

OMEGA: Yes. But that is just another of the fairy tales this race is so fond of using in coming to terms with its reality. Actually, the Aquarians were so impressed with what seemed to them the awesome powers of the Andorians that they worshiped us as a multi-faced god who had come down from the heavens to participate in the affairs of men. This superstition, this delusion, has continued, as you no doubt know, until the present time.

ALPHA: I am familiar with the god-image our brothers projected upon the population. But you will have to fill me in on the other details of our intervention.

OMEGA: Well, it is a tale soon told. The D-Team's misguided efforts enabled the Aquarians to make great strides in intellectual and material achievements, but there was no spiritual awakening and the race consciousness remained stunted and immature.

In the course of many centuries the search mission finally located a black hole that might be used as an exit. However, after much testing its energy potential proved to be too weak for a transitional passage. Then a desperate, momentous decision was made. At the behest of Roaldic, the senior fleet advisor, our brothers determined to attempt the unthinkable—the deflection of Aquarius from its orbit into the vicinity of the cosmic crack so that its gravitational energy could be used as a booster.

ALPHA: I know, of course, that the orbital diversion was successful and that it was masterminded by Roaldic, who had to convince his comrades that such a maneuver was possible. But I am not familiar with the celestial mechanics involved. Can you enlighten me on this point?

OMEGA: The operation was rather simple in concept

but extremely complex in execution. Only a genius of Roaldic's caliber could have brought it off.

Our spaceships have two kinds of power: electromagnetic for propulsion and antigravitic to neutralize the attractive force of matter. Roaldic stationed four of the ships in stationary orbits above the surface of the planet facing its sun, thereby shielding most of its area from the gravitational force of the primary. The fifth ship was similarly stationed on the sun side of the satellite, which screened its entire surface from the star's attractive force.

As I said, the concept was a simple one. With the star's gravitational force on the planet drastically reduced, its own inertial velocity would carry it into a larger orbit. When this orbit reached the vicinity of the cosmic crack, it was only necessary to discontinue the shielding operation and Aquarius would stabilize in its new orbit. In this way the planet moved itself 892,900 miles farther from the sun at a velocity of about 248 miles per hour in 150 days of local time. But it was a ticklish operation. The satellite had to be controlled in its orbit of Aquarius and the planet, itself, was subjected to devastating floods and other cataclysms.*

It was fortunate that Roaldic had the foresight to transfer the planet's inhabitants and representatives of all other air-breathing species to a preconstructed base inside the satellite. When Aquarius was finally stabilized in the new orbit, our brothers returned its former inhabitants in toto. Then—

ALPHA: But what about Noah's Ark which, according to the scripture of an important religious sect, managed to

---

*For a more detailed explanation of this momentous change in the earth's orbit, see Chapter 11 of the author's previous work, *UFOs: The Extrauniversal Connection* (Exposition Press, 1977).

save only one family while salvaging representatives of every other air-breathing species?

OMEGA: I was coming to that. The Aquarians were subjected to such traumatic experiences during the orbital diversion they rejected the entire episode and substituted a fairy tale involving Aquarian wickedness and their God (the D-Team) to account for the "Deluge," as it came to be called.

This tale, which appears in the first book of the scripture you referred to, is quite ingenious, and for that reason I will quote excerpts from it.

"And God saw that the wickedness of man was great in the earth . . . And it repented the Lord that he had made man . . . And the Lord said, 'I will destroy man whom I have created from the face of the earth; both man and beast and the creeping thing, and the fowls of the air; for it repenteth me that I have made them . . . And, behold, I, even I, do bring a flood of waters upon the earth to destroy all flesh, wherein is the breath of life, from under heaven; and everything that is in the earth shall die.' "

To account for the survival of life forms after the Flood, this writer employed a clever literary device:

"But Noah found grace in the eyes of the Lord: 'With thee I will establish my covenant; and thou shalt come into the ark, thou, and thy sons, and thy wife, and thy sons' wives with thee . . . And of every living thing of all flesh, two of every sort shalt thou bring into the ark, to keep them alive with thee; they shall be male and female' . . ."

A side effect of this substitution of fantasy for reality, this blotting-out process, was their reversion to the primitive state in which we found them. In other words, they managed to shed the thin veneer of material progress fostered by the D-Team, and even the vast store of new knowledge acquired during the intervention was buried deep within their subconscious. I suppose this was just as well for they were, and are, headed in the wrong direction.

Naturally, we were anxious to return to our own dimension after such a lengthy absence but, as a salve to our conscience, we took the time to program the D-Team to remain permanently at the moon base and keep the Aquarians under surveillance. After our return to Andor and after a great deal of experimentation, we were able to establish a transuniversal communication link with the D-Team. This, plus periodic visits by members of the A-Team, provides us with an accurate record of Aquarian development, or lack of it. But, of course, you are familiar with our intelligence network.

ALPHA: Yes. And from what I have learned during my study of the Aquarian problem, your description of the species as a carnal, superstitious, naked ape is as relevant now as it was in the past. Perhaps even more so, for the data received from our sources indicate mental and physical turmoil in all areas of life, particularly the political and religious. The roots of these disturbances reach back to the period of our intervention, which you have described. In my view we have a moral responsibility to take whatever steps we can to halt and reverse their flight down the road of ignorance and superstition. The situation has now reached a critical stage and strong measures are called for.

OMEGA: Do you have any particular course of action in mind?

ALPHA: Indeed I have and I will get to that in a moment.

I have learned that any attempt to manipulate the psyche of a species is a precarious undertaking. Your report confirms this. We have failed once, a failure attributed to the physically oriented D-Team, and we have no assurance the A-Team would have fared any better.

Therefore, another overt intervention cannot be justified. It is my thinking we should give them the blueprint for a harmonious reality and let them work out their own salvation. If we attempt to do it for them—as was the case in our original experiment—they will learn nothing and gain nothing of lasting value.

I believe the best approach would be through their religious beliefs. There is a very active religious sect known as Israelites, or Jews, who believe their God will send a Messiah to deliver them from their Roman oppressors and establish a utopian kingdom on the planet. Because of its traditions and the authority accorded its scriptural prophecies, this sect is convinced the advent of a savior is imminent. As we know, this God concept originated with the Andorian intervention, which spawned a system of mythology that eventually attained the status of a full-blown religion. This religion maintains that the God who once desired to destroy his creation by flood is now planning to send his personal emissary to save man from himself. This is not only a paradox, but it provides additional evidence of the Aquarian proclivity for superstition and self-delusion. It also sets the stage for a bold new experiment.

OMEGA: You intrigue me. Please continue.

ALPHA: I have called it a bold experiment but it may border on the impossible—a word we do not ordinarily accept at face value. We must somehow insert a highly developed entity into the Aquarian milieu who will have a ready-made opportunity to teach them the truth on their own level of understanding.

OMEGA: In other words you are advocating covert intervention by a single individual as opposed to the massive overt intervention of the past when our space fleet was stranded in the Aquarian system. And, furthermore, you feel that such a project could successfully indoctrinate an entire race.

Tell me, Alpha, what are your reasons for believing that one Andorian can succeed in such a mission when an entire fleet of our brothers failed so dismally?

ALPHA: There are three reasons. One—during the overt intervention our brothers were prevented from bringing their best efforts to bear on the problem due to the exigencies of the black hole mission, whereas our single individual can devote his entire time and attention to the matter at hand. Two—in the overt intervention our brothers were viewed as an outside agency with godlike powers that should be deified, and, thus, the Aquarians could not relate to them on a personal basis, whereas our single emissary will be accepted as one of them, as an extraordinary member of their own race in whom they can place their confidence and trust. Three—the first experiment was largely conducted by low-level, physically oriented entities, whereas the contemplated mission will be carried out by a highly developed being.

OMEGA: It is a risky undertaking that will generate its own complexities and pitfalls and no doubt will tax our resources. While the risk to us is minimal—involving the fate of only one Andorian—it is a gamble that could determine the future course of an entire race for either good or ill. But the audacity of your plan appeals to me and presents a challenge worthy of our best minds.

Now, tell me, how do you propose to implement this unique project of yours?

9

The "Immaculate Conception"

Now the birth of Jesus Christ was on this wise: When as his mother Mary was espoused to Joseph, before they came together, she was found with child of the Holy Ghost.—The Gospel of Matthew

(We continue to monitor this strange dialogue.)

ALPHA: The first step, of course, is to insert a high-level Andorian into the Jewish culture in a natural and un-obtrusive way. For obvious reasons, any attempt to introduce a strange adult into such a tight-knit society would be self-defeating. We must, therefore, start with a newborn or even a prenatal child.

OMEGA: I don't quite follow you. Please explain.

ALPHA: Both methods have advantages and disadvantages. At the moment I feel the prenatal procedure holds the greatest promise of success. But I will outline both for your evaluation.

The newborn child procedure must depend in large measure on fortuity. And that is a built-in weakness. First, we would have to locate a newly married Jewish couple with the proper lineage. Then we must wait until the wife is pregnant with a male child. Then, when she is delivered, we must have an Andorian midwife on hand to switch babies— leaving one of ours in the cradle and returning to us with the Jewish infant.

This procedure is riddled with hazards, some of which cannot be foreseen. Too much must be left to pure chance. In addition, we just don't know which would prove to be dominant in the aging process—qualities outside the body or within it. We have never had occasion to check this out. But I feel intuitively that the gene-carried longevity component is dominant. If this is the case, we would be faced with an anachronism: a child who takes so many AQ years to develop and mature that his contemporaries would all be dead before he could even begin his mission. Furthermore, such a pro- longed life span would mark our emissary as being so differ- ent from other mortals as to suggest the supernatural and invite deification. This is what occurred in our previous inter- vention, and we would not want that to happen again.

In my opinion, this factor alone tips the scales against baby-switching. What is your thinking?

OMEGA: I agree that this method leaves much to be desired. Now, let's have the prenatal procedure.

ALPHA: It is fairly simple and leaves very little to chance.

As before, our first step is to locate a Jewish couple with

the proper lineage. This must be done before intercourse has taken place for reasons that will become apparent.

While the search is going on, we will prepare a male gender fertilized egg from an Andorian couple of the highest order. I would suggest Roaldic as the sperm donor. We will retard the longevity gene in the egg by either laser or chemical means so that the child will develop even more rapidly than his coevals.

OMEGA: I think I can see where this is leading, but please continue.

ALPHA: When the signal is received from our intelligence sources that the necessary betrothal has occurred, we will dispatch an appropriate team to Aquarius with the fertilized egg. The success of the entire project hinges upon a simple but delicate operation performed during a single nighttime hour.

Before that time comes, our special team will have infiltrated the neighborhood masquerading as members of a caravan en route to market with its merchandise. In this way they will arouse no suspicion and can circulate freely among the people.

The team will maintain a careful watch over the home of the bride-to-be. When the time is auspicious and the household has settled down for the night, specialists will steal into the house and immobilize everyone in it. Our surgeon will then implant the fertilized egg in the future bride's womb. Mission accomplished, the team will board a hovering spaceship for the return flight to Andor.

OMEGA: Your plan is unfolding beautifully. Let's hope it will continue to do so.

ALPHA: I am optimistic, but the final decision must rest with you.

10

The "Lost Years"

The laws of mind are the laws of reality.—Arthur M. Young

(The canonical Gospels as well as the Apocrypha are strangely silent concerning that period in the life of Christ between the age of twelve, when he engaged the doctors in a learned discussion in the temple at Jerusalem, and the age of thirty, which marked the beginning of his ministry. These years are accounted for as the Andorian dialogue continues.)

OMEGA: You have suggested a remarkable course of action, and I see no reason at the moment why it should not succeed. But I have some questions. As this child grows up, how is he to know his true identity and what is expected of him? Even if he knew this much, he still would know nothing of our philosophy and would be of no use to us as an emissary. Have you considered this difficulty?

ALPHA: Yes, I have. In all modesty I must confess I have thought this operation through from beginning to end. But to answer your questions. When the child has reached the approximate age of twelve AQ years, he will already be a prodigy in every sense of the word, capable of absorbing vast amounts of knowledge very quickly.

We will bring him to Andor and reveal to him his real identity and purpose on Aquarius. We will then subject him to a crash course in our philosophy and metaphysics, plus a review of Jewish traditions.

OMEGA: How long will this take? And will not his absence cause anxiety and suffering for his family?

ALPHA: By using nonstop instruction, whether he is awake or asleep, we can indoctrinate the boy in about eight weeks. It will be another week or ten days before we can put him back on Aquarius. This is approximately eighteen years of AQ time, a considerable period on the planet. And it is important that such a time lapse be accounted for in a normal fashion. We will, therefore, put an A-Team on Aquarius (or Earth, if you prefer) disguised as teachers and holy men. They will ingratiate themselves with the boy's parents and convince them that such a precocious child should be placed in their custody for advanced instruction and preparation for a life of service to mankind. I have no doubt the parents will feel both honored and proud to have their offspring regarded as a personage of such great importance and will gladly agree to such an arrangement. They will let it be known their son has been sent to a far country to take advantage of educational facilities not available in his own land. Thus, an absence of some years can be justified.

OMEGA: It would appear you have anticipated every contingency and I am favorably impressed. But I have one final question. What methods will our emissary employ to indoctrinate the populace?

ALPHA: He will use oral teaching techniques that are compatible with the times to reach as many listeners as possible. Because of the primitive nature of the Aquarian culture, he will be able to reach only a small portion of the population in this manner. Therefore, it is essential that he should recruit a number of close associates, or disciples, who can spread the word over a period of time throughout the world.

When our emissary has done everything possible to teach the truth in this manner, we will consider his mission terminated and bring him back to Andor.

Now, with your permission, I will put this plan into effect.

OMEGA: You have my blessing and best wishes.

(Eight Andorian weeks later we are again privileged to tune in on a top-level meeting in progress. This time a third person is present. The co-leaders address him as Jesus, and, as he responds to his interrogators, it becomes evident he has been groomed for a role that demands an expertise verging on perfection.)

OMEGA: Now that you know the truth, concerning your identity and purpose on Aquarius, Jesus, what are your feelings? Do you, perhaps, harbor the impression that you are being used?

JESUS: I feel no more like a pawn than any other who does not ask to be born, who must live in a world not of his own making and whose death comes unbidden. On the contrary, I consider it an honor to be the one chosen to carry out a mission of such profound importance to all mankind. It is with humility and a sense of high purpose that I embark upon the course you have set.

ALPHA: You speak of "any other who does not ask to be born," and so on. How do you reconcile such a statement with our metaphysics?

JESUS: I do not attempt to reconcile the two. I was speaking from the standpoint of the Aquarian, or earthling, who so believes. We know that every soul carries within itself dominion over all manifestation including birth of the body, the conditions of life, and physical death. Actually, the body and experiential reality are constructs of mind, the creative power within. Even the Book of Genesis, which is primarily based on myth, manages to express this verity in somewhat ambiguous terms. You will recall that in the first chapter of the book God tells man to have dominion over the earth and everything in it. This is another way of saying that man is responsible for his total reality. And it will be my task to lead Homo sapiens to an acceptance of this truth.

Like every other expression of consciousness, I alone am responsible for being who, what, and where I am, and I have no desire to evade that responsibility.

OMEGA: Spoken like a true Andorian. Now, according to Alpha, your program of instruction covered three broad areas that are essential to your mission. They are: (1) Jewish mythology and traditions; (2) Aquarian, or human, history and psychology; and (3) Andorian philosophy and the nature of reality. Can you tell me why I listed them in that order?

JESUS: The first two are stepping-stones to the third. As the expected Jewish Messiah, I must be letter-perfect in the "law and the prophets" of their religion; as a member of the Aquarian race, I must be familiar with its history and the forces that motivate the individuals in it. This background is necessary before I can effectively teach our philosophy and metaphysics.

Fortunately, I was thoroughly versed in the first two areas before your team brought me to Andor. Thus, I have been able to concentrate on the third area, which is the be-all and end-all or, if you will pardon the expression, the Alpha and Omega of my mission.

ALPHA: I am sure Omega will agree with me that you have used an appropriate term to describe the thrust of your assignment. Now, tell me, how do you plan to enlighten a race so steeped in ignorance and superstition? How will you deal with a devoutly religious sect whose beliefs and forms of worship are so firmly entrenched?

JESUS: If it were not for this sect's anticipation of a Messiah, I would suggest that we direct our efforts toward a more flexible and influential caste such as the Romans. But the Jewish milieu provides an opportunity and a challenge unique in human history.

I must impersonate their Messiah and convert them by using contemporary religious terms in a new way. I must begin with the known and familiar and lead them into the strange and the unknown. This can best be done by employing metaphors and parables that will reveal new truths hidden beneath the murky waters of their dogma.

To be accepted, new ideas must be presented in a familiar framework. For example, the Creative Power resident in consciousness will be referred to as the Kingdom of God or of heaven. And, again, the inception of a harmonious reality will be described in such simple terms as "Do unto others as you would have them do unto you," and "Love thy neighbor as thyself." Stories about everyday life will be used to illustrate the points I wish to make.

And, finally, I will perform "miracles" by creating illusions to dramatize my message and render it unforgettable. Everything I say and do will be calculated to drive home a single truth: Mind is the creator, reality the created.

OMEGA: The Jews are an uncommonly pious people and, as such, they spend much time praying to their God. Formal prayers for specific occasions and purposes are an essential part of their devotions. Do you have any ideas on how this custom can be turned to our advantage?

JESUS: After giving this matter much thought, I feel I have reached a satisfactory solution. I have taken our own universal prayer as a model. To make my point, I will repeat it verbatim.

"Great Spirit—Designer and Creator of the body in which we dwell, in and through which we live and move and have our being:

"Cause us to realize that the perfect pattern for all manifestation is contained in consciousness; that anything less than perfect expression is the result of wrong thinking and wrong application of Universal Law; that the Creative Power that fashioned the universe is resident in our consciousness, ready to serve us at any time of need; that as creatures of free will, we can control this creative power and direct it for the highest good of all. So be it."

I have converted this prayer to a colloquial form, which conveys the same great truth in terms more readily understood by those addressed, as follows:

"Our Father which art in heaven, Hallowed be thy name. Thy kingdom come, thy will be done in earth as it is in heaven. Give us this day our daily bread. And forgive us our debts, as we forgive our debtors. And lead us not into temptation, but deliver us from evil: For thine is the kingdom, and the power, and the glory, forever. Amen."

ALPHA: Your Aquarian prayer is beautifully simple and even shorter than ours, yet in essence its meaning is the same. It is, indeed, a masterful composition. Roaldic will be proud of you. Now, we are open to any questions you may have.

JESUS: I know that I am to use oral teaching methods, for this is traditional with the Jewish savants and prophets. Nevertheless, I have a feeling it would be prudent to have my teachings recorded in writing. After all, they are a radical departure from the accepted doctrine and subject to misconstructions.

OMEGA: I believe you can use your time and energy to better purpose by reaching as many listeners as possible while, at the same time, indoctrinating a select group of disciples who can carry your teachings throughout the planet. As your close friends and trusted confidants, their conversion will be total and, having attained to the proper degree of consciousness, their recall should be faultless. Although your message is new, it is quite simple and should be easily understood by the average man. On the other hand, if you depend on a written record to preserve your teachings, there is the possibility of its being altered in copying or translation, or even lost entirely.

ALPHA: I agree with Omega. In our own history memory has proved superior to all other forms of record keeping. Memory is tamper-proof and not subject to the hazards that plague written material. We never make mechanical records of our sessions here. They are indelibly inscribed upon our memory banks.

Is there anything else, Jesus?

JESUS: Yes, there is. I would remind you that I will be dealing with a barbarous race whose values are entirely different from ours. Many things take precedence over human life, among them status, power, wealth. I have a premonition the Jewish religious hierarchy will view my message as a threat to its authority and will take whatever measures are necessary to stay in power—even to killing the messenger. Have you considered these dangers?

OMEGA: Since your mission has been Alpha's brainchild from the beginning, I will refer that question to him.

ALPHA: I feel that provisions have been made for every contingency.

In the first place, a member of the team which engineered your conception remained on the planet as an undercover agent. Over the years he has established himself as a rich and respected counselor of the Jewish community. He is aware of the dangers confronting you, and your welfare will be his major concern. He is known to the Jews as Joseph of Arimathea, and you will come to know and rely on him during the course of your ministry.

If an emergency arises and Joseph is unable to help you, you are to employ telepathy to contact our base in the moon. They will relay your message to us here and we will take appropriate action. Remember that telepathic messages can be transmitted with greater clarity late at night and from an isolated locality.

Are you satisfied with our arrangements for your welfare?

JESUS: I can find no fault with them. Now the time for action has come. Let us begin.

11

The Garden of Gethsemane

A man must be both stupid and uncharitable who believes there is no virtue or truth but on his own side.—Addison

The accuracy of Jesus' premonition that his mission and even his life would be imperiled by reactionary religious leaders became increasingly evident as his ministry approached its climax. The time was now at hand to follow Alpha's instructions and alert the satellite outpost to the necessity for prompt action by his sponsors on Andor. Even his staunch comrade, Joseph of Arimathea, would be powerless to combat the forces arrayed against him. But before employing such extreme measures, he would call his disciples together for a farewell supper and prepare them for future developments.

A description of this "last supper" can be found in the canonical Gospels as well as a rendering of the events which followed in an isolated area later that night. With the fore-knowledge that Jesus was using the power of thought to com-municate his plight to his fellow Andorians, we read the following account in the twenty-sixth chapter of Matthew with some astonishment:

> Then cometh Jesus with them unto a place called Gethsemane, and saith unto the disciples, "Sit ye here, while I go and pray yonder."
>
> And he took with him Peter and the two sons of Zebedee, and began to be sorrowful and very heavy.
>
> Then saith he unto them, "My soul is exceeding sorrowful, even unto death: tarry ye here, and watch with me."
>
> And he went a little farther, and fell on his face, and prayed, saying, "O my Father, if it be possible, let this cup pass from me: nevertheless not as I will, but as thou wilt."
>
> And he cometh unto the disciples, and findeth them asleep, and saith unto Peter, "What, could ye not watch with me one hour? Watch and pray, that ye enter not into temptation: the spirit indeed is willing, but the flesh is weak."
>
> He went away again the second time, and prayed, saying, "O Father, if this cup may not pass away from me, except I drink it, thy will be done."
>
> And he came and found them asleep again: for their eyes were heavy. And he left them and went away again, and prayed the third time, saying the same words.
>
> Then cometh he to his disciples, and saith to them,

"Sleep on now, and take your rest: behold, the hour is at hand, and the Son of Man is betrayed into the hands of sinners. Rise, let us be going: behold, he [Judas] is at hand that doth betray me."

Matthew's Gospel goes on to relate how Jesus was arrested, brought to trial for blasphemy and condemned to death.

But the point to be made here is the clumsiness of Matthew in his account of the praying Jesus at Gethsemane. At the very least it smacks of fabrication. Matthew admits that Jesus walked some distance from the three disciples and "fell on his face and prayed." If Jesus prayed in a loud voice, a practice he condemned in others, his utterances would still have been muffled and hardly intelligible at a distance. Matthew further admits that during the session of prayer Jesus returned to the disciples three times and each time found them asleep. The conclusion is inescapable: neither the sleeping disciples nor anyone else could have known the content of Jesus' prayers. Yet Matthew, in spite of all evidence to the contrary, claims to know every word Jesus spoke or thought.

This is another example of the lengths to which biblical writers were prepared to go in order to conceal their ignorance of the true nature of events. Jesus did not pray either vocally or silently; rather, he was employing all the mental power at his command to communicate with his brother Andorians. The outcome of these efforts will be revealed in the following pages.

12

The Resurrection

The voyage of discovery consists not in seeking new landscapes, but in having new eyes.—Marcel Proust

Curiously enough, the same three clues appear in all four canonical Gospels, which suggest that some outside agency was at work during and after the crucifixion of Christ. Matthew, Mark, Luke, and John give substantially similar accounts in reporting these crucial events, which can be recognized by the informed reader as evidence of discreet Andorian intervention.

The first clue is the nameless individual who "ran and took a sponge, and filled it with vinegar; and put it on a reed, and gave him [Jesus] to drink." Almost immediately Jesus cried with a loud voice and "yielded up the ghost." Was this so-called vinegar really a powerful drug that could simulate death in the man on the cross?

The second clue is the role played by Joseph of Arimathea, whom we recognize as an Andorian undercover agent. Luke gives this account:

"And, behold, there was a man named Joseph, a counsellor; and he was a good man, and a just: (The same had not consented to the counsel and deed of them); he was of Arimathea, a city of the Jews: who also himself waited for the Kingdom of God.

"This man went unto Pilate, and begged the body of Jesus. And he took it down [from the cross], and wrapped it in linen, and laid it in a sepulchre that was hewn in stone, wherein never man before was laid."

This was the opportunity Joseph needed to revive Jesus with sophisticated Andorian medical techniques.

The third clue involves either one or two strangers (the Gospels are not consistent on this point) who were discovered by Mary Magdalene and Mary the mother of James in the empty tomb of Christ. Here is Luke's version of the incident:

"Now upon the first day of the week, very early in the morning, they [the women] came unto the sepulchre, bringing the spices which they had prepared, and certain others with them. And they found the stone rolled away from the sepulchre. And they entered in, and found not the body of the Lord Jesus.

"And it came to pass, as they were much perplexed thereabout, behold, two men stood by them in shining garments: And as they were afraid, and bowed down their faces to the earth, they [the men] said unto them, Why seek ye the living among the dead? He is not here, but is risen. . .”

As might be expected, Matthew's report of the incident is more dramatic:

“In the end of the sabbath, as it began to dawn toward the first day of the week, came Mary Magdalene and the other Mary to see the sepulchre. And, behold, there was a great earthquake: for the angel of the Lord descended from heaven, and came and rolled back the stone from the door, and sat upon it.

“His countenance was like lightning, and his raiment white as snow: And for fear of him the keepers [those guarding the tomb] did shake, and became as dead men. And the angel answered and said unto the women, Fear not ye: for I know that ye seek Jesus, which was crucified. He is not here: for he is risen. . .”

The Gospel writers never mention the strangers in white again, leaving the reader to wonder who they were and why they showed themselves at all.

It is a reasonable assumption that Christ's Andorian rescuers took compassion on his family and friends and sought to assure them that their Messiah was not really dead but had risen and returned from whence he had come. This is a reasonable deduction as opposed to the mythical resurrection and later purported appearance on earth of a risen Jesus, as described by the Gospel writers. These authors realized that a religion based on a crucified individual who then mysteriously disappeared, never to be heard from again, would be no religion at all. Perhaps a philosophy of life could be developed from his ministry, but not the kind of religion with a supernatural nimbus these zealots were determined to establish.

Let us now turn to the Apocryphal Gospel of Peter, which is more enlightening than all the orthodox Gospels put together. We pick up the narrative at the point where Jesus is being crucified:

> Now it was *midday* and a *darkness* covered all Judaea. And they became anxious and uneasy lest the sun had already set, since he [Jesus] was still alive. For it stands written for them: the *sun* should not *set* on one that had been put to death. And one of them said, "Give him to drink *gall* with *vinegar.*" And they mixed it and gave him to drink. And they fulfilled all things and completed the measure of their sins on their head. And many went about with lamps, and as they supposed that it was night, (they went to bed or they stumbled). And the Lord [Jesus] *called out and cried,* "My power, O power, *thou hast forsaken me!*" And having said this he was taken up. And at the same hour *the veil of the temple* in Jerusalem was rent *in two.*
>
> And then the Jews drew *the nails* from the hands of the Lord and laid him on the earth. And the whole *earth shook* and there came a *great fear.* Then the sun shone (again), and it was found to be the ninth hour. And the Jews rejoiced and gave his body to Joseph that he might bury it, since he had seen all that he [Jesus] had done. And he took the Lord, washed him, *wrapped him in linen* and brought him into his own sepulchre, called Joseph's *Garden.*
>
> Then the Jews and the elders and the priests, perceiving what great evil they had done to themselves, began to lament and to say, "Woe on our sins, the judgment and the end of Jerusalem is drawn nigh." But I mourned with my fellows, and being wounded in heart we hid ourselves, for we were sought after by them as evildoers and as persons who wanted to set fire to the temple. Because of all these things *we were fasting* and sat *mourning and weeping* night and day until the Sabbath.

But the scribes and Pharisees and elders, being assembled together and hearing that all the people were murmuring and beating their breasts, saying, "If at his death these exceeding great signs have come to pass, behold how *righteous* he was!"—were afraid and came *to Pilate,* entreating him and saying, "Give us soldiers that we may watch his sepulchre *for three days, lest his disciples come and steal him away* and the *people* suppose that he *is risen from the dead,* and do us harm." And Pilate gave them Petronius the centurion with soldiers to watch the sepulchre. And with them there came elders and scribes to the sepulchre. And all who were there, together with the centurion and the soldiers, *rolled* thither a great stone and laid it against the entrance of the sepulchre, and *put* on it seven *seals,* pitched a tent and kept watch. Early in the morning, when the Sabbath had dawned, there came a crowd from Jerusalem and the country round about to see the sepulchre that had been sealed.

Now in the night in which the Lord's day dawned, when the soldiers, two by two in every watch, were keeping guard, there rang out a loud *voice in heaven;* and they saw the *heavens opened* and two men *come down* from there in a great brightness and draw nigh to the sepulchre. That *stone* which had been laid against the entrance to the sepulchre started of itself to roll and gave way to the side, and the sepulchre was opened, and both the young men entered in. When now those soldiers saw this, they awakened the centurion and the elders—for they also were there to assist at the watch. And whilst they were relating what they had seen, they saw again three men come out from the sepulchre, and two of them sustaining the other, and a cross following them; and the heads of the two reaching to heaven, but that of him who was led of them by the hand overpassing the heavens. And they heard a voice out of the heavens crying, "Thou has preached to them that sleep," and from the cross there was heard the answer, "Yea." Those men therefore took council with one another to go and report this to Pilate. And whilst they were still deliberating, the heavens were again seen to open, and a man descended and entered into the sepulchre. When those who were of the centurion's company saw this, they hastened by night to Pilate, abandoning the sepulchre, which they were guarding, and reported everything that they had seen, being full of disquietude and saying, "*In truth* he was *the Son of God.*" Pilate answered and said, "I am clean *from the blood* of the Son of God, upon such a thing have you decided." Then all came to him, beseeching him and urgently calling upon him to command the centurion and the soldiers to tell no one what they had seen. "For *it is better* for us," they said, "to make ourselves guilty of the greatest sin before God than to fall into the hands of the people of the Jews and be stoned." Pilate therefore commanded the centurion and the soldiers to say nothing.

Early in the morning of the Lord's day *Mary Magdalene,* a woman disciple of the Lord—for *fear* of the *Jews,* since (they) were inflamed with wrath, she had not done at the sepulchre of the Lord what women are wont to do for those beloved of them who die—took with her her women friends and came to the sepulchre where he was laid. And they feared lest the Jews should see them, and said, "Although we could not weep and lament on that day when he was crucified, yet let us now do so at his sepulchre. *But who will roll away for us the stone* also that is set *on the entrance to the sepulchre,* that we may go in and sit beside him and do what is due?"—*For the stone was great*—"and we fear lest any one see us. And if we cannot do so, let us at least put down at the entrance what we bring for a memorial of him and let us weep and lament until we have again gone home."

> So they went and found the sepulchre opened. And they came near, *stooped down* and saw there *a young man* sitting in the midst of the sepulchre, comely and *clothed with a brightly shining robe,* who said to them, "Wherefore are ye come? *Whom seek ye?* Not him that *was crucified? He is risen* and gone. But if ye believe not, stoop this way and *see the place where he lay, for he is not here.* For he is risen and is gone thither whence he was sent." Then the women *fled affrighted. . . .* *

Although it is obvious Peter was honestly reporting all that he saw, it is also obvious he had no understanding of what was taking place. His ignorance of the true nature of these events matches that of the primitive Pacific island natives who deified the "white gods" of the U.S. bomber squadron during World War II. He was as mystified by this display of UFO phenomenon as the author of Exodus, who used similar terms to describe the intervention of an outside agency in the flight of the Jews from Egypt.

Peter was an awed and bewildered witness of the Andorian rescue operation whereby two A-Team members descended from a luminous spaceship on a beam of light, retrieved Jesus from the tomb, and gave him expert medical care aboard the craft. A third Andorian entered the tomb for another purpose: to reassure those who sought the crucified Christ. This is the entity described by Matthew in his canonical Gospel and by Peter in his Apocryphal Gospel as the one who came down and frightened the soldiers and later spoke to the women in the sepulchre. In the confusion that followed

*From *New Testament Apocrypha,* Volume One, edited by Wilhelm Schneemelcher and Edgar Hennecke. English translation edited by R. McL. Wilson. Published in the U.S.A. by The Westminster Press, 1963. Copyright © 1959 J. C. B. Mohr (Paul Siebeck), Tübingen. English translation © 1963 Lutterworth Press. All footnotes, paragraph, and verse numbers appearing in the original have been omitted. Used by permission.

he was taken aboard the hovering spacecraft, which then returned with Jesus and his rescuers to Andor.

By simple deduction we can draw the conclusion that Jesus recuperated on Andor; that he and his sponsors were dismayed by the unforeseen consequences of his mission; and that they analyzed every aspect of his ministry in an effort to understand why and how it failed in its purpose. It also can be deduced evidentially that this superior race is no longer motivated to redeem mankind.

This last deduction is valid in spite of a widespread belief in the "Second Coming" of Christ. This belief is based on passages in the Synoptic Gospels, which represent Jesus as saying he would return to earth "in the clouds of heaven with power and great glory" after the world had suffered many tribulations. Such believers apparently ignore the qualifying passage in all three Gospels where Jesus says, "Verily I say unto you, this generation shall not pass, till all these things be fulfilled." Needless to say, that generation passed away many centuries ago. And, further, it is quite probable that this portion of the Synoptics was marred by erroneous reporting and interpretation, a defect all too common in the Scriptures.

Then there are the UFO buffs who may ask, "If the Andorians are no longer interested in saving man from himself, why all the UFO activity reported since the crucifixion of Christ?" They must be reminded that such activity can be attributed to the D-Team operating from its concealed base beneath the surface of the moon.

13

The Right-Hand Door

In the preceding pages we have offered an alternative to established beliefs, and the open-minded reader may recognize it as being more reasonable and plausible than Christian doctrine. He may even agree it makes more sense to understand the message and act upon it than to worship the messenger. And that is where the trouble lies, for intelligence has never been a requisite for the followers, or even the leaders, of any religious movement. In fact, the skeptic, the independent thinker, is an unwelcome goat in any flock of believing sheep. Yet, in the final analysis, any improvement in the human condition must come from the heretics. The sorry plight of our world today is a massive indictment of an ineffectual Christianity. This is hardly surprising in the framework of a belief system that pays homage to the God of Genesis and glorifies human sacrifice. In the opinion of this writer, sincere and dedicated heretics are the only hope for a psychic rebirth that could revolutionize the mental concepts of a race flirting with disaster.

We are all familiar with religious road signs carrying such messages as "Jesus Saves," "Hell and Damnation Await the Unbeliever," and "Christ Loves You" ad nauseam. One such sign observed recently was more thought-provoking. Beneath the message "Jesus is the Answer," someone had added this graffiti, "What is the question?" Those four words are more profound than all the canons of Christendom. It is axiomatic that to get the right answer, one must ask the right question. For centuries the Christian has been asking the wrong question. He has been asking how he can prevail upon someone else to "save" him, when he should be asking what he can do to save himself. He has been his own worst enemy.

To put it another way, the Christian edifice has two doors. Behind the left-hand door stands the deified figure of Christ, the Savior of all believers. Behind the right-hand door lies a mystery since the believer has never dared to open it. He has been content to swallow an antiquated doctrine and follow the herd through the left-hand door sanctified by venerable dogma and pious homilies.

Apropos to the door analogy is the series of experiments performed by Prof. N. R. F. Maier of the University of

Michigan in which "neurosis" is induced in rats, as reported by S. I. Hayakawa in *Language in Thought and Action*.

The rats are first trained to jump off the edge of a platform at one of two doors. If the rat jumps to the right, the door holds fast, and it bumps its nose and falls into a net; if it jumps to the left, the door opens, and the rat finds a dish of food. When the rats are well trained to this reaction, the situation is changed. The food is put behind the other door, so that in order to get their reward they now have to jump to the right instead of to the left. (Other changes, such as marking the two doors in different ways, may also be introduced by the experimenter.) If the rat fails to figure out the new system, so that each time it jumps it never knows whether it is going to get food or bump its nose, it finally gives up and refuses to jump at all. At this stage, Dr. Maier says, "Many rats prefer to starve than make a choice."

Next, the rats are forced to make a choice, being driven to it by blasts of air or an electric shock. "Animals which are induced to respond in the insoluble problem situation," says Dr. Maier, "settle down to a specific reaction (such as jumping *solely* at the left-hand door) which they continue to execute regardless of consequences. . . . The response chosen under these conditions becomes fixated. . . . Once the fixation appears, the animal is incapable of learning an adaptive response in this situation." When a reaction to the left-hand door is thus fixated, *the right-hand door may be left open so that the food is plainly visible.* Yet, the rat, when pushed, *continues to jump to the left,* becoming more panicky each time. When the experimenter persists in forcing the rat to make choices, it may go into convulsions, racing around wildly, injuring its claws, bumping into chairs and tables, then going into a state of violent trembling, until it falls into a coma. In this passive state, it refuses to eat, refuses to take any interest in anything: it can be rolled up into a ball or suspended in the air by its legs—the rat has ceased to care what happens to it. It has had a "nervous breakdown."*

Over one-third of the human race, including the elite in all walks of life, is fixated on the left-hand door of Christianity. This door gives access to an intermediary who, according to sacrosanct doctrine, is capable of remitting all sins and ushering the believer into heaven. This is as attractive to the mentally lazy, the wishful thinker, as is the reward of food to the hungry rat. What could be more appealing to this branch of Homo sapiens than effortless, instant "salvation"?

Behind the right-hand door there is no outside agency of any kind, only complete mental and spiritual freedom to apprehend the creative process by which all men can be brought into harmony with their fellows, their world, and their universe. This is the kind of harmony Jesus had in mind when he said, "I am come that they might have life, and that they might have it more abundantly." He knew that no thing, no person is an isolated entity. Everything that exists is interrelated in a nonmaterial, all-inclusive field of consciousness. This field of consciousness is manifested in patterns of energy that take form and substance in accord with the laws of mind. An understanding of these laws will enable us to divine the process of creation and our role in the dynamism of that process.

*From *Language in Thought and Action,* Fourth Edition by S. I. Hayakawa, copyright © 1978 by Harcourt Brace Jovanovich, Inc. and reprinted with their permission.

Jesus sought to teach this maxim by using such metaphors as "The Kingdom of God is within you"—a reference to the creative power residing in consciousness which fashioned the universe and stands ready to serve any human need. "If thou canst believe," he said, "all things are possible to him that believeth." A passage in Proverbs expresses the same idea: "As a man thinketh in his heart, so is he." To which we might add, "and so is his world." And who can argue with this statement, "He that ruleth his spirit is better than he that taketh a city."

The brilliant astronomer and physicist, the late Sir James Jeans, recognized the nonmaterial nature of reality when he asserted that the universe begins to look more like a great thought than like a great machine.

Behind the right-hand door is Plato's "world of reality" as opposed to the visible world of appearance, illusion, and decay. He was saying that the real world—the realm of thought—is indestructible while the energy patterns it produces are transitory. Behind this door lies another Garden of Eden where man can "come to himself" and reclaim his birthright as co-creator of his own ambience. He can implement the message of Jesus and use his innate mental and psychic powers to create and control an experienced reality forged in his own best interest. Here is the blueprint for a better life, a better world for all of humanity in the here and now—a world whose determinants originate on the mental plane.

It is the rare individual indeed who possesses the intellectual curiosity to open this door and the spiritual stamina to explore the consciousness-expanding challenges beyond its portals.

For many centuries Christians have been incapable of

learning an adaptive response to the two-door situation. They are too easily discouraged by a bump on the nose from the closed right-hand door. Even if the door is open and the vistas beyond are plainly visible, they continue to jump to the left regardless of the consequences to themselves and to their world.

They have not yet understood or accepted the symbolism of the two ways as taught by Jesus. Instead of "door," he used the word "gate"; in place of "left and right," he used "wide and strait." Here is the Master's message according to Matthew:

"Enter ye in at the strait gate: for wide is the gate, and broad is the way, that leadeth to destruction, and many there be which go in thereat: Because strait is the gate, and narrow is the way, which leadeth unto life, and few there be that find it." (Matt. 7:13-14)

14

Christianity, Cults, and Magic

*And if Christ be not risen,
then is our preaching vain,
and your faith is also vain.—St. Paul*

As noted in Chapter 12, the New Testament writers realized that a religion based on a crucified individual who then mysteriously disappeared from his tomb, never to be heard from again, would not provide the magical and miraculous elements needed to capture the minds and emotions of the people. It was absolutely essential, therefore, to establish beyond doubt by every means available that Christ bodily rose from the dead and ascended to heaven. The Christian monolith has been built on this single miraculous event and depends upon the constant reinforcement and proliferation of this doctrine for its survival.

No one understood this better than St. Paul who was converted from a persecutor of Christians to a powerful advocate in the early stages of the movement. A sophisticated Roman citizen and a product of the Greek-Hebrew culture, Paul became an eloquent and indefatigable proselytizer of the struggling new faith. He became the catalyst that propelled a tiny, obscure cult into the forefront of the world's great religions.

His letters and sermons were the real beginning of the attempt to formalize, rationalize, and put down in orderly argument the Christian faith. His influence was so great it has been charged that Paul, not Jesus, is the real author of what we know today as Christianity.

In his role as architect, advocate, and proselytizer of a belief system based on the miraculous and the magical, Paul became the precursor of modern evangelism. Self-anointed ecclesiastics link Pauline dynamism and charisma with the electronic media to sell the Christian bill of goods to millions around the globe. This spiritual exploitation has become big business, reaping billions of dollars annually from the pockets of the gullible. St. Paul never had it so good.

The modern phenomenon of cultism has also taken a page from Paul's book on conversion and translated his fanatical techniques into a subtle but vicious form of brainwashing. Factions such as the Unification Church, Hare Krishna, Children of God, Church of Scientology, Divine Light Mission, est, Peoples Temple, Silva Mind Control, PTL, and Transcendental Meditation—to name only a few among thousands—pose a pervasive threat to our society as a whole by transforming converts into unfeeling, unaware, non-thinking zombies.

These cults, which arose in the sixties and early seventies, have gulled millions of followers with the promise of release from life's restrictions and expansion of the human potential. Such "enlightenment" can only be achieved by blind adherence to the tenets of the particular cult, which take their cue from self-serving interpretations of Judeo-Christian teachings. These sects have become rich and powerful through sophisticated mass-marketing strategies and continuous recruitment by devotees. According to one authority on the subject, the cult movement is the greatest threat and danger to this country it has ever had to face. "But," he says, "the people won't wake up . . . until something bad happens."

As everyone knows, many bad things have already happened in the name of religion. One is reminded, for example, of a nit-picking theological dispute in the early Christian church which caused millions of men, women, and children to be maimed, mutilated, and murdered—graphically illustrating the "Three Ms" of Western religion.

Less obvious but just as real in the context of Christianity is a fourth "M," which denotes Magic. Since this faith embraces theurgical magic—divine or supernatural intervention in human affairs—it should come as no surprise that magic rituals are routinely performed in every Christian church. Let's examine these rituals as they are described in a scholarly work on this aspect of religion.

> To begin with, the same basic patterns run through both those rituals labeled religious and those labeled ceremonial magic in Western culture. In fact, the word "ritual" comes from a Latin root related to "number"

or "counting," the way things are to be done (that is, "one after another"). Since "ceremony" is equivalent to "ritual" for our purposes here, ceremonial magic is just magic with the emphasis on the ritualistic aspects. In all rituals the crucial point is to do things in the proper order in the proper way, usually as prescribed by custom or tradition. . . .

Despite their more abstruse theological differences, most of them totally unknown to their believers, the churches known as "Protestant" . . . have retained for the most part the basic order of worship perfected by the early Greek and Roman Catholic churches. Let us attend one now.

We see the priest or minister entering upon the sacred area at the front of the church. He goes before the altar and begins to address prayers in the general direction of various geometric shapes or statues. In Catholic churches, these are often pictures or statues of Christ crucified, Mary, Joseph, or other saints; for ritualistic purposes, these are far superior to the more bare (and often barren) symbols that others use. These opening prayers usually consist of confessions of past offenses and requests that the deity addressed will (a) not hold it against them, and (b) listen to the prayers to follow. The congregation often joins vocally or silently in these prayers.

Passages are then read from various books; most presumed with brave and noble disregard for facts to the contrary to be the handiwork of the god in question. Thus, the deity in effect replies to the prayers just offered.

Then a sermon is preached emphasizing some theological point deemed of interest or importance, but requiring neither intelligence nor action from the congregation. Here of course the basket is passed.

The officient returns to the altar and resumes his

dialogue with the god, presenting him with gifts, especially bread and wine. In the early centuries of the Christian era, all the members of the congregation would have marched up and presented actual loaves of bread and jugs of wine. It was also at this point that new converts would have been dismissed because they were not worthy to witness the miracle to come. But back to the twentieth century.

The priest now identifies himself with the god by repeating the incantation that turns the bread and the wine into the body and blood of the god. It is very important that we note that the priest says, "This is *my* body . . . this is *my* blood" and not "This is *your* body . . . this is *your* blood" as would be the case in a mere commemoration. If you are a Catholic, this is a literal change called *transubstantiation;* if you are a Protestant, this is a symbolic change called *consubstantiation . . .**

Now the congregation and the priest consume the now-tangible god, believing that in doing so they will absorb his powers and characteristics (this is in addition of course to the virtues of sharing food with one another). After the meal is over, the deity is thanked for coming down, and his presence in the communion is reaffirmed. Final prayers and requests are made by the now powerful and god-filled congregation. The minister tells the people that their prayers will be granted, that the god is with them, and then dismisses them.

Throughout the ceremony [particularly in Catholicism], all sorts of props, costumes, music, incense, and miscellaneous special effects are used to heighten audience emotions to a peak that culminates with the

---

*It was this theological hairsplitting that brought about the atrocities in the early church previously cited.

consecration and consumption of the god-food and subsequent wielding of his powers. Though some of the prayers are altruistic, most are for pragmatic everyday blessings upon crops, children, property, and so on. . . .*

This author goes on to describe rituals of the rain dance performed by the Hopi Indians; the snake handling ritual of the White Pentecostalist Church in southern Tennessee; the Voodoo ceremonies in Haiti; and other magical rituals used by little-known sects and cults across the U.S.

It would seem that everybody is trying to get into the act, and that the difference between Christian ritualistic magic and that of other religious factions is a matter of degree rather than of kind. They are all after the same thing: favors from their god and identification with him. In every case formalized rituals are used to achieve these ends. Some are characterized by solemnity and moderation, as in Christianity; others are more extreme and boisterous, as in Voodooism and the antics of Holy Rollers.

Throughout the centuries magic and religion have vied for the loyalties of men. As magic (and its attendant superstitions) appeared on the scene first with its miraculous and supernatural mystique, it presented a formidable obstacle to early religions—especially to a struggling and obscure Christianity. This now powerful sect owes much of its success to a very simple premise: "If you can't beat 'em, join 'em."

We have seen how Protestants and Catholics alike still employ ritualistic magic in their worship services. But the very beginnings of Christianity were based on an unabashed

*Reprinted by permission of Coward, McCann & Geoghegan, Inc. from *Real Magic* by Philip Emmons Isaac Bonewits. Copyright © 1971 Philip Emmons Isaac Bonewits.

adaptation of pagan magic. This is evident in the Gospel descriptions of the miracles performed by Jesus. Parenthetically, it should be noted that these accounts were recorded many years after Christ's ministry.

A pagan philosopher and magician named Apollonius was born in the Asia Minor city of Tyana during the very early years of the Christian era. He became well-known as a healer and clairvoyant and was said to be a master of illusion. But beneath all the romance there appears to be the outline of a genuine historical figure.

Apollonius became popular with the pagans of Rome at the time that Christianity was gaining strength. Many miracles were ascribed to him which parallel those attributed to Jesus—such as the miracle of the loaves and the fishes, the raising of Lazarus, changing water into wine at the wedding feast, and walking upon water. All of these were magical feats and were readily accepted by pagans of whatever persuasion. In fact, some anti-Christian writers drew direct parallels between the life of Jesus and that of Apollonius of Tyana, a comparison which enraged the early Christians.

What is one to make of all this? For one thing, it is abundantly clear to the objective observer that religion of every kind is dependent upon the miraculous and the magical to keep its faith alive and viable. As man came first in the scheme of things and is responsible for whatever religion there is, he has himself injected these elements into his dogma. It is he and not some unearthly agency who keeps his gods alive and their dominion over the minds of men intact. This is the way it always has been and will continue to be as long as people prefer fantasy to reality.

At this stage in the human experience, one is inclined to conclude that what the world needs most is a rational religion.

A specious belief system is quite insidious. Almost imperceptibly it generates distortions inimical to a healthy, sane, and mature society.

At one time in recent history the attainment of religious freedom was hailed as a great step forward. It turns out that such an achievement has only given men the latitude to make ever greater fools of themselves. A more meaningful advance would be the assumption of personal accountability and the concept of freedom *from* religion.

As noted earlier, Jesus himself throughout his ministry challenged all formal and legalistic religion while proclaiming that inner virtue mattered more than outward conformity to mere rules of behavior.

Postscript

In all generations the nonconformist, the self-motivated individual, has been the catalyst in human affairs, the activator in every major advance. The modern world of sophisticated technology could not function or hardly exist without the invention of the wheel by some prehistoric genius. The mass of humanity owes an incalculable debt to this unknown innovator and to other exceptional individuals with such names as da Vinci (multigenius), Michelangelo (sculptor/painter/architect/poet), Copernicus (astronomer), Newton, (philosopher/mathematician), Edison (multiinventor), Bell (telephone), Goddard (rocketry), Ford (autos/assembly line production), the Wright brothers (aviation pioneers), and Einstein (physicist) whose unorthodox ideas and vision changed the world.

With rare exceptions no group, no commission, has ever come up with anything of lasting value. Even the devout Christian can appreciate the extraordinary individual and give thanks to his God who so loved the world that he didn't send a committee. It has been said that the camel is the ludicrous product of a committee given the task of designing a horse.

The Bureaucracy, the agency, the commission, the entrenched Establishment (both secular and religious) are magnified versions of the inept committee with the common denominator of mediocrity. We would qualify this indictment by quoting the remark of an admired professor of literature at our alma mater: "No general statement is always true, including this one."

Conceding that truth may be relative, we still maintain that deference to the majority in the important areas of life is a cross we all must bear and, no doubt, prompted Thoreau to say that the mass of men lead lives of quiet desperation. The stultifying tyranny of numbers creates a condition where the blind are leading the blind and contributes to the meaningless existence decried by that nature-loving philosopher.

Lives that are devoid of challenge and any real purpose other than that of acquisitiveness are a damning commentary on the kind of Christianity that holds us hostage. The outmoded doctrine that ensnares us is a religious camel created over the centuries by self-appointed groups, councils, and committees who have had a vested interest in the grotesque creature they sired.

Subservience to this kind of doctrine has taken us down the path of quiet desperation. It has led us through the wide gate and down the easy road that leads to hell. We have nothing to lose and everything to gain by making a new path and leaving a well-marked trail for others to follow. It will take us through Jesus' strait gate into the narrow way that leads to life—a more abundant life for all. Can there be any higher calling than that of trailblazer?

If this book has motivated the reader to go where there is no path in the religious jungle and to discover the narrow way, he will find a brotherhood of kindred spirits crying in the wilderness whose voices will one day be heard and heeded. What are they saying? They are calling our attention to this little-known truth: *When a myth is shared by large numbers of people, it becomes a reality.* Millions of Christians are living in their own version of reality.

One final note. Numerous volumes filled with trivia flood bookstores each year. They provide ample evidence that any fool can write a book, and many do. But only the Great Spirit can make the trees from which their pages come. Is this work worthy of the tree? The reader must make that judgment for himself.

Bibliography

Anderson, Charles C. *The Historical Jesus: A Continuing Quest.* Grand Rapids, MI: William B. Eerdmans Publishing Co., 1972.

Atmore, Anthony and other contributors. *The Last Two Million Years —A Reader's Digest History of Man.* New York: The Reader's Digest Association, 1974.

Bonewits, P. E. I. *Real Magic.* New York: Coward, McCann & Geohegan, Inc., 1971.

Buttrick, George Arthur (ed.). *The Interpreter's Bible.* The Holy Scriptures in the King James and Revised Standard Versions with General Articles and Introduction, Exegesis, Exposition for Each Book of The Bible. Twelve Volumes. New York: Abingdon Press, 1952-1957.

Caldwell, Taylor and Jess Stearn. *I, Judas.* New York: Atheneum Publishing, Inc., 1977.

Cameron, James W. *The Bible—Infallible Guide: Truth or Myth.* New York: Carlton Press, 1974.

Conway, Flo and Jim Siegelman. *Snapping.* New York: Dell Publishing Co., 1979.

de Chardin, Teilhard. *The Phenomenon of Man.* New York: Harper & Row, 1965.

————. *The Future of Man.* New York: Harper & Row, 1969.

Dione, R. L. *Is God Supernatural? The 4,000-Year Misunderstanding.* New York: Bantam Books, 1976.

Fuller, R. Buckminster. *And it Came to Pass—Not to Stay.* New York: Macmillan Publishing Co., 1976.

Funk & Wagnalls Standard Encyclopedic Dictionary. *The World's Religions.* New York, 1975.

Gaer, Joseph. *What the Great Religions Believe.* New York: Dodd, Mead, 1963.

Geyer, John. *The Wisdom of Solomon (Apocrypha).* London: SCM Press, Ltd., 1963.

Goodspeed, Edgar J. *The Apocrypha: An American Translation.* New York: Vintage Books, 1959.

__________. *How Came the Bible?* New York: Pillar Books, 1976.

Harkness, George. *The Modern Rival of Christian Faith.* Nashville, TN: Abingdon-Cokesbury Press, 1952.

Hayakawa, S. I. *Language in Thought and Action.* New York: Harcourt, Brace, 1949.

Hennecke, Edgar, edited by Wilhelm Schneemelcher. English translation edited by R. McL. Wilson. *New Testament Apocrypha, Vol. I.* Philadelphia: The Westminster Press, 1963.

__________. *New Testament Apocrypha, Vol. II.* Philadelphia: The Westminster Press, 1976.

Hick, John, editor. *The Existence of God.* New York: The Macmillan Co., 1964.

Holy Bible, King James Version. Cleveland: The World Publishing Co.

Jauncey, James H. *Science Returns to God.* Grand Rapids, MI: Zondervan, 1961.

Jewett, B. (trans.). *The Works of Plato.* New York: Tudor Publishing Co., undated.

Levi. *The Aquarian Gospel of Jesus the Christ.* Santa Monica, CA: Devorse & Co., 1972.

Percival, Harold W. *Thinking and Destiny.* New York: The Word Publishing Co., 1946.

Perrin, Norman. *Jesus and the Language of the Kingdom. Symbol and Metaphor in New Testament Interpretation.* Philadelphia: Fortress Press, 1976.

Potter, Charles Francis. *The Lost Years of Jesus Revealed.* Greenwich, CT: Fawcett Publications, 1962.

Russell, Bertrand. *Why I Am Not a Christian.* New York: Simon and Schuster, 1957.

Schonfield, Hugh J. *The Passover Plot.* New York: Bantam Books, 1967.

__________. *Those Incredible Christians.* New York: Bantam Books, 1968.

Sproul, R. C. *Knowing Scripture.* Downers Grove, IL: Intervarsity Press, 1977.

Steiger, Brad. *Words from the Source. A Metaphysical Anthology of Readings from the Louis Foundation.* Englewood Cliffs, NJ: Prentice-Hall, 1975.

Stromberg, Gustaf. *The Soul of the Universe.* Laguna Hills, CA: Educational Research Institute, 1965.

————. *The Searchers.* Los Angeles, CA: Science of Mind Publications, 1977.

Thompson, Frank Charles. *The New Chain Reference Bible.* Indianapolis: B. B. Kirkbride Bible Co., 1964.

Throckmorton, Burton H., Jr. (ed.) *Gospel Parallels, A Synopsis of the First Three Gospels* (2d ed., rev. 1957). New York: Thomas Nelson & Sons, 1965.

Time, Inc. *The World's Great Religions.* New York: Life, 1957.